MW01101462

DIAMOND
IN THE
ROUGH

DIAMOND
IN THE
ROUGH

A Refining 40-Day Devotional Journal

TRACY XAVIER

DEDICATION

This book is dedicated to my treasures,
Sophia Grace and Serena Jolie.
I pray you will always see yourselves
as nothing short of God's incredible handiwork.
I am thankful everyday to our Heavenly Father,
who gave me two such precious gifts.
I love you with all my heart.

For my mom, Ligaya,
who is absolutely beautiful inside and out.
Thank you for instructing me in the way I should go.
I love you, Miss Happy.

SPECIAL THANKS

My deepest appreciation to the Lord Jesus,
for speaking these prayers over me,
and for constantly displaying His true love.

Pastors Jack and Joyce Holt,
thank you for being mighty examples
of faith and grace in action.
I praise God for giving me
"pastors according to His heart."

And to my husband and best friend, Jim.
Thank you for being a man of God, a student of the Word,
and one who loves the Holy Spirit.
You are amazing in more ways than I could describe,
and I'm forever grateful for you.

DIAMOND IN THE ROUGH
TABLE OF CONTENTS

DIAMOND IN THE ROUGH
TABLE OF CONTENTS

DIAMOND IN THE ROUGH

Although the phrase has been around for almost 400 years, the first time I can actually recall hearing it used was in the Disney animated movie "Aladdin." In case you haven't seen it, let me paint this picture: Aladdin is a pauper who, by a series of mishaps, meets a beautiful princess posing as a peasant girl. Meanwhile, an evil sorcerer, desperate to strip the sultan of his ruling powers, attempts to retrieve a magic lamp from the Cave of Wonders. He learns he must first find the one who is called "The Diamond in the Rough" in order to gain entrance to this extraordinary cavern. It is discovered that Aladdin alone holds the ability to unlock secrets and treasures held within the mystical cave. The boy who believed he would forever live as a 'street rat' uncovered his true identity through overcoming a series of nasty trials and unfortunate circumstances. A diamond in the rough he was. I probably don't need to tell you that he indeed married the princess and lived happily ever after. Sorry for the spoiler, but you probably expected that finish!

We may not be living the fairy tale, and we may be miles from the 'happily ever after' to our own stories. But one similarity holds true to us all: we are diamonds in the rough. To be compared metaphorically to the original, unpolished state of a diamond gemstone, particularly that which has the potential to become a high-quality jewel, is a very befitting description of us as women, and especially appropriate for those of us who have committed our lives to serving and loving Jesus Christ.

As we seek to know God intimately, we often reflect on His attributes and the many names by which He reveals Himself: *Jehovah Jireh* - the Lord our Provider; *Jehovah Rophe* - the Lord our Healer. We also consider the ways in which the Bible describes the infinite characteristics of Jesus: *the Alpha and the Omega, the Beginning and the End, the Bright and Morning Star.* Meditating on the magnitude and grandeur behind the names of God manifests a sense of His greatness. As we ponder the meaning and truth behind the names and descriptions of God, we are held in awe of who He knows Himself to be. But the question I ask of you is this:

**Have you ever contemplated how God
has characterized *you?***

This isn't an exercise in exhibiting pride or boastfulness. On the contrary, if we fail to understand — and believe according to His Word — who God called us to be, we can never truly give God the credit or the glory for His most magnificent creation. He called you and me to be the temples in which His Holy Spirit would dwell. If we cannot envision ourselves as one of the most tremendous displays of His handiwork, then we fail to see God as Master Creator.

THE DIAMOND DECLARATION

The Bible says in Hebrews 4:12 that "the Word of God is living and powerful, sharper than any two-edged sword," and that it exposes our innermost thoughts and desires. How true we find this to be when we study and meditate and pray the Word of the Living God. We are also told in Proverbs 18:21 that "death and life are in the power of the tongue, and those that love it will eat its fruit." I want the entire Word of God to be living and active in my life, and I believe you do, too. For this reason, we must not only be hearers of the Word, although hearing is good. We must be active in doing the Word, and that includes *declaring it, confessing it, speaking it, decreeing it — saying it — out loud and with our mouths.*

Something glorious ignites within our spirit when we hear the heart of God speaking to us; we know He's alive, that He's personal, and that His desire is for us to draw close. He is calling us to a place of love and power to live in His presence in order to demonstrate love to all whom we meet.

God Almighty has given us great purpose in Him, and I want you to receive this truth and allow it to forge deep into your heart. On the following page is a set of verses I want to share especially with you. One day several years ago, during a very difficult and dry season, I had awakened one morning with an urgency to challenge this spiritual slump I was in. The Lord led me to Ephesians 1:3 and from there, delivered a message of encouragement through His Word that even today, lifts my spirits. These scriptures were not written in succession in the Bible itself, but the entire of Word of God weaves a singular message of love that can hardly go unnoticed once we begin to dig, dig, dig.

THE DIAMOND DECLARATION

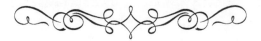

"Blessed be the God and Father of our Lord Jesus Christ, who has blessed us with every spiritual blessing in the heavenly places in Christ, just as He chose us in Him before the foundation of the world, that we should be holy and without blame before Him in love,
Ephesians 1:3-4

who has saved us and called us with a holy calling, not according to our works, but according to His own purpose and grace which was given to us in Christ Jesus before time began,
2 Timothy 1:9

For we are His workmanship, created in Christ Jesus for good works, which God prepared beforehand that we should walk in them.
Ephesians 2:10

...being confident of this very thing, that He who has begun a good work in you will complete it until the day of Jesus Christ;
Philippians 1:6

The Lord will perfect that which concerns me; Your mercy, O Lord endures forever; Do not forsake the work of Your hands."
Psalms 138:8

It is my prayer that you will commit these verses to memory and begin to declare them over your own life. In God's mind, He already knew exactly what He planned for us to accomplish on this earth, not only before we were born, but before He created the world! The thought is overwhelming, and yet it is absolutely true.

THE INVITATION

Before we begin this journey, we must come to an agreement and understanding about the Word of God: that everything written in God's Word concerning His people *will* come to pass. We should make no mistake about it.

> *"For as the rain comes down, and the snow from heaven,*
> *And do not return there,*
> *But water the earth,*
> *And make it bring forth and bud,*
> *That it may give seed to the sower*
> *And bread to the eater,*
> **So shall My word be that goes forth from My mouth;**
> **It shall not return to Me void,**
> **But it shall accomplish what I please,**
> *And it shall prosper in the thing for which I sent it."*
> *Isaiah 55:10-11*   *(emphasis, mine)*

If we look at the above verses, we see three things. First, God compares a natural law of earth with the spiritual law of heaven. Just as the earth naturally operates within God's sovereign design, so does His supernatural word operate as He specifically intended. A well-watered seed planted in good soil, under just the right weather conditions can't do anything BUT grow. The seed has no say in the matter. It must operate under the natural, scientific laws of agriculture. But how does the supernatural law of God's forth-going Word apply to us? There's a variable here that doesn't exist with the first example, and that's the issue of free will. God gave us the freedom to accept or reject His word, the freedom to believe or disregard the gift of grace offered to us through His son, Jesus. **The growing in this case depends on our cooperation in working with God's Word through faith.** Please don't miss this very foundational point. Without an understanding of this groundwork, the benefits from this devotional will be minimal. However, if you go into these next 40 days with a heart ready to receive based on *believing in faith*, then you will begin to see Jesus at work in a wonderful way.

The second point I'd like for you to see through the previous scripture is that the benefit of growth is not simply for growing. God's intention for growth is not solely for personal enlightenment, but to accomplish much deeper purposes. In the case of the seed, it is to provide more "seed to the sower" and "bread to the eater." God has an end-goal in mind for the harvest which will result from the sprouting seeds. Likewise, your growth directly affects your purpose on this planet. As you begin to take hold of who you are according to God's Word, you will begin to see God's intent and design for you. You were created to directly affect the world around you, to be a person of influence in the lives of those God has put in your path.

And lastly, let's look at Isaiah 55:11 again, *"So shall My word be that goes forth from My mouth; It shall not return to Me void, But it shall accomplish what I please, And it shall prosper in the thing for which I sent it."* Does this mean that God's Word will accomplish everything in your life for which He intends? Yes, it does. However, your faith is what makes the difference. Faith, spiritually speaking, is a verb, not a noun. It cannot sit and just "be." It must be active, it must be doing something! If you believe in God's Word, you will act on it. You will not let it sit on the pages of the Bible for someone else. You will receive it for yourself and begin to line your personal actions in accordance with that Word.

Here's an example of this verse in action: imagine

preparing a lavish party. You've dreamt time and again of throwing such a bash – gathering your closest friends, giving them an opportunity to meet one another. Each of your friends come from every imaginable background and, as one would expect, all are incredibly fascinating and talented (well, of course they are, they're *your* friends, after all!). You can't wait for these electrifying personalities to occupy the same room while they enjoy themselves, exchange ideas and share outrageous stories! You take great care to deliver your invitations, anticipating that all will gladly accept.

It's the day of the party. You scan your mental check list, assuring every detail is covered. Spotless house? Check. Table, seating, perfect atmosphere? Check. Food and beverages are yummy and ready for serving? Check. Beautiful hostess? Check! What could go wrong? At the last minute, you discover several guests declined your invitation. One girlfriend called and said she had other commitments that day; another friend decided at the last minute to stay home and didn't give you any reason at all. Still another friend decided not to come because she - now, get this - really didn't think you wanted her there. *Well, the nerve! How could they?* Despite your disappointment, the party ensues and you can confidently (and yes, with all humility) boast it truly was a monumental evening. It was unfortunate that those who declined missed out. Long after the event, your friends who attended still regard it as the party of the year.

God's Word is His invitation to you. It's an invitation to experience abundant life, amazing peace, unmistakable joy, blessings beyond your imagination – in essence, THE most amazing party of all time! He desires for all who receive the invitation to respond with a *yes,* but there are those who simply don't believe His invitation is worth the response. There are those who deny that God truly cares whether they're "in attendance" or not, although nothing could be further from the truth. His Word will certainly accomplish all that He intends, but whether you are a recipient of that intent is your decision.

You are God's chosen, his delight, his precious girl! He accepted you into His royal family when you believed in the atoning death of Jesus Christ, and accepted His free gift of eternal life. That alone qualifies you as an heir to the kingdom. Just as the daughter of an earthly king would be entitled to her father's estate and all his goods, how much more entitlement do we receive from our loving, eternal Father?

SEEING THROUGH THE EYES OF FAITH

When I crawl out of bed in the morning, I can easily report to you this is not my best, nor my favored, look. Aren't we thankful for toothbrushes, deodorant, cleanser, hair products, and running water? Don't get me wrong: after the morning hygiene ritual, there are those who can get away with the toss-and-go hairstyle and the bare-naked face, though I'll admit I've never been a toss-and-go kind of gal (unless I'm desperate to fulfill a craving and have to head to the nearest grocery store). I'm grateful for the transformation I personally execute and witness before my bedroom mirror each day, from the first stroke of eyeliner to the last dab of lipstick. If I had the misfortune of being stranded on a deserted island, somehow I'd make sure a supply of moisturizer and mascara were handy, in the event of a possible rescue!

I'm also forever thankful that the Lord looks far beyond our exterior into the depths of our heart. His eyes see not only where we are today, but our entire lives from before we were born to the exhaling of our last earthly breath – and beyond. We are called to set our mind on things above (Col 3:2) and to see things the way God sees, from His divine perspective. His vision is set on things of eternal value, and that includes the workings of our inner being. Without the eyes of faith, we cannot see that we are highly valuable, much more than what mirrors reveal. The eyes of faith allow us to entertain dreams we've never shared with a single soul; longings and yearnings that others may find extreme and outright ridiculous. The Lord delights in us, His daughters, and I believe He longs to see us walking in the light of who He created us to be. He sees each of us as absolutely breathtaking, full of godly wisdom, dispensing grace and mercy to all who are in need of a true touch of heaven here on earth.

Let us speak words of life over our own lives, over our very being, putting Proverbs 18:21 into daily action. In the pages to come you will find 40 days of devotions. They are written as prayers, and several are written as declarative confessions, in a voice I hope you will use as your own. Make a commitment within your heart to the Lord that you will take some time out of each day for 40 consecutive days to make these verses and prayers yours, speaking them out loud in faith. You will also find questions or suggestions that accompany each day, called *Facets*. As you spend time answering the questions with pen in hand or participate in the daily tasks, you will be putting feet to your faith in each days' devotional.

Somehow, it seems much easier to believe with others for their healing, or offer encouragement to those who need a kind word or a listening ear. It's true that as daughters in Christ, we should do these things, and that God blesses those who serve others with a pure heart. But oftentimes we find it difficult, sometimes even (dare I say it) impossible to have faith for our own situation, or find encouragement when we feel alone. The truth is, you are never alone, and there is One who cares more than anyone ever could! God's Holy Spirit dwells within you and He is just waiting for you to get into this book and take this journey with Him!

Do you see yourself as God has described you in His Word? Do you see yourself as strong, blessed - as a woman of influence? Do you see yourself as healed, whole, and free? Let's encounter the Word together, and discover this gem - the *you* God created. As you begin to unveil the brilliance, beauty, and truth behind God's most precious possession, I pray that the eyes of your heart would also open to a new level of power, confidence, and passion through the Holy Spirit.

DAILY DEVOTIONS

DAY 1

I AM BLESSED

"Blessed be the God and Father of our Lord Jesus Christ, who has blessed us with every spiritual blessing in the heavenly places in Christ, just as He chose us in Him before the foundation of the world, that we should be holy and without blame before Him in love…"
Ephesians 1:3-4

"Blessed is the man You choose,
And cause to approach You,
That he may dwell in Your courts.
We shall be satisfied with the goodness of Your house,
Of Your holy temple."
Psalm 65:4

"Blessed are those who dwell in Your house;
They will still be praising You."
Psalm 84:4

"Blessed is every one who fears the LORD,
Who walks in His ways.'"
Psalm 128:1

I DECLARE TODAY:

I am blessed with every spiritual blessing. Because I am the daughter of the Most High God and King, I am entitled to everything that my Father possesses. He bestows only His best upon me. He has given me the most priceless gifts imaginable – reconciliation and redemption through the shed blood of His most precious Son, Jesus. Because of my Father's intense love for me, I am committed to reflecting His love to all with whom I come in contact. I am His representative on earth, an ambassador charged with the divine call of demonstrating His compassion and mercy to a needy and dying world.

As the daughter of the Almighty, I am in possession of all that belongs to Him: His riches; His glory; His authority; His power; His strength; His wisdom, and His peace. He has given me everything that pertains to life and godliness. His Word compels me to press beyond what I see in the natural in order to grasp what is mine in the Spirit.

I declare that I am a woman who is blessed and highly favored. God's deep love for me is proven through the gift of Jesus, and through the anointing of the Holy Spirit. I now receive all that my Heavenly Father has generously granted me, in Jesus' Name. Amen.

FACETS

◊   What does the blessing of the Lord look like to you? On the accompanying page, make a list of ten blessings you have received within the past year. Write ten more you would like to see within your life over the next year.

◊   Ask the Lord for something you've not yet requested of him. Write a prayer just below your list of blessings.

DAY 2
I AM STRONG

"Cast thy burden upon the Lord, and He shall sustain thee: He shall never suffer the righteous to be moved."
Psalm 55:22 KJV

"But those who wait on the LORD shall renew their strength; they shall mount up with wings like eagles, they shall run and not be weary, and they shall walk and not faint."
Isaiah 40:31 KJV

MY PRAYER FOR TODAY:

Heavenly Father,

I declare that my strength is in You and You alone. You are my strong tower and refuge. In You I find all that I need to continue living a life of peace, a life of grace, and a life of love and mercy toward others.

Without You, I can do nothing – but with You, I can do all things! I can accomplish every task and purpose for which You've assigned to me. I can do the impossible because You are resident within me and I seek to abide in You. I look to You, Lord, my complete source of holy power! There is no limit, no lack in You, Lord. Therefore, I have within me everything needed to do all that I am called to do! I rely on Your strength; I wait for Your manifestation of grace in order to exhibit Your life. You provide the means to accomplish this. With You, I am strong and empowered to live out Christ's example here on earth. You did not create me to live in defeat, nor did You create me to live in a state of helplessness and in isolation. With Your Holy Spirit residing in me, I have all that is necessary to live out a life of true power.

Help me daily to tap into the strength that is within You, Lord. As I remain in Your Word, and dedicate myself to Your ways, I believe You will continue to supernaturally energize and recharge me to complete every good work.

I declare this by faith in Jesus' Name. Amen!

FACETS

◊   Before the Israelites took possession of the promised land, the Lord told the people through Moses to "remember well what the Lord Your God did to Pharoah and to all Egypt." God also encouraged the people by explaining that He would drive out the nations before them little by little - not all at once. The Israelites needed to increase in strength and in number in order to overcome predators who would consume them if they were to remain alone in the wilderness.

◊   The Lord wants us to remember well our previous victories in order to remain strong for current or future trials. He wants to make Himself well known to us during our wilderness experiences. Can you relate to the concept of gaining victory day by day, or even moment to moment? Read Exodus 23:20-31 and Deuteronomy 7 and jot down any interesting parallels to your own experience.

◊   Recall a time in your life when you pulled through a difficult situation or overcame a hardship. Did you recognize God at work through this period? How did he use you or another person during that time?

DAY 3
I AM TREASURED

"Now therefore, if you will indeed obey My voice and keep My covenant, then you shall be a special treasure to Me above all people; for all the earth is Mine."
Exodus 19:5

"For you are a people holy to the LORD your God. The LORD your God has chosen you out of all the peoples on the face of the earth to be his people, his treasured possession."
Deuteronomy 7:6

"This mystery is that through the gospel the Gentiles are heirs together with Israel, members together of one body, and sharers together in the promise in Christ Jesus."
Ephesians 3:6

MY PRAYER FOR TODAY:

     Mighty Father, I praise You for Your infinite vision and ways that move far beyond my own limited thinking. How grateful I am, Lord, that You have grafted me into Your family and now call me Your treasured possession – a peculiar treasure, unlike anything else in all world! Where would I be without the blood of Jesus that brings me into a right-standing relationship with You? I profess that a moment in Your presence brings me greater fulfillment than a lifetime of accomplishment without You! How amazing it is, Lord, that You desired to be with me so much, that You gave Your one and only son as payment for my sins; that I am now righteous in Your sight, and not only that, but treasured.

     Your love is incorruptible and completely perfect. It is selfless, forever giving, fierce, and yet altogether tender. It is a love that I crave deeply, and it thoroughly washes over me when I draw near to You. Your love for me is undeniable. In times when I feel lost and overwhelmed, cause me to recall this fierce and tender love You have toward me, Your child. In times of persecution and pressure, turn my heart toward thoughts of patience, endurance, and the long-suffering You've shown me. In times of joy, help me to remember that You are the source of it all. How great is this love, Lord! Let that declaration emanate from all that I am. Let me be found in You always.

     In Jesus' precious Name, I pray. Amen.

FACETS

◊   What is one rare thing you hold dear to your heart? A childhood memento? Memories of a lost loved one? Describe this treasured possession of yours. Afterward, take a moment to reflect on how much more God treasures YOU.

DAY 4
I AM FULL OF POTENTIAL

" 'For who has known the mind of the Lord that he may instruct him?' But we have the mind of Christ."
1 Corinthians 2:16 KJV

"This mystery has been kept in the dark for a long time, but now it's out in the open. God wanted everyone, not just Jews, to know this rich and glorious secret inside and out, regardless of their background, regardless of their religious standing. The mystery in a nutshell is just this: Christ is in you, so therefore you can look forward to sharing in God's glory. It's that simple."
Colossians 1:26-27 The Message

MY PRAYER FOR TODAY:

Your Word declares that You knew me long before I was born, that You numbered every one of my days before they came to pass. You alone hold the mysteries of the universe, and You alone know the depths of my heart. You alone know my desires, my dreams, all of my thoughts, motives and intentions. As I seek to be transformed by renewing my mind, to walk toward Your perfect will for my life, I submit every negative pattern of thinking to You. I call them out for what they are: corrupt, false, damaging, and malicious. I understand that engaging in negative thoughts and distorted modes of thinking are Satan's method of operation to gain advantage over me. His only intent is to steal what is rightfully mine – spiritual gifts and unhindered fellowship with my Heavenly Father.

I will no longer accept the deceptive whisperings of the enemy and I give the evil one no ground, no place for him to plant seeds of death within my mind. I reject the lies that the devil would speak over me, and I cast down every imagination that exalts itself against the knowledge of Christ. You call me the apple of your eye, Your beloved child; therefore, I choose to believe You. I also make the choice to accept Your calling in my life: to be holy, spotless, and blameless before You in love. I realize this is only possible because of the wonderful work finished on the Cross.

As I commit my mind to you, I ask that You would make known Your presence in unprecedented ways. I thank You in advance for heavenly dreams and for words of wisdom to flow from your Holy Spirit into my inner man. I thank You for revelation, and for divine timing orchestrated in my life. I look forward to blossoming in Christ, and I'm thrilled at all that You are accomplishing within me. Thank You for revealing the awesome potential I have in You, for You are not only at work in me, You live in me!

I have all victory in Jesus' Name! Amen.

FACETS

◊   Picture a powder keg or a box of dynamite. The outer shell isn't particularly threatening, yet the potential and impact of what lies within is literally life-altering. If the powder keg sat untouched, well, nothing would happen of course! In a positive manner, consider your potential with Christ inside of you. In what ways could you impact life with Jesus fully in control?

◊   What would you like to yet accomplish during your lifetime?

DAY 5
I AM PROSPEROUS

"Beloved, I pray that you may prosper in all things and be in health, just as your soul prospers…"
3 John 1:2

"Grace and peace be multiplied unto you through the knowledge of God, and of Jesus our Lord, According as his divine power hath given unto us all things that [pertain] unto life and godliness, through the knowledge of him that hath called us to glory and virtue…"
2 Peter 1:2-3 KJV

MY PRAYER FOR TODAY:

Dear Heavenly Father,

You have already given me every good and perfect gift. There was not one thing lacking when you sent Jesus to die in order that He might bring me into a right relationship with You. His flawless sacrifice made the way for me to receive Your perfect gifts of forgiveness, peace, and joy. All these and so much more are mine, therefore, I am a prosperous woman. You have already provided the knowledge and wisdom I need in order to live a life fulfilled. I receive all these good and perfect gifts which You created before the foundations of the earth.

I thank You for them, and as a good steward I choose to operate in all the gifts which You have given me. These gifts make me a prosperous woman. There is nothing I can't accomplish through You. As I choose to abide in Christ, I understand that I may ask of You anything that I desire, and that in You, all Your promises are yes and amen. Thank you, Lord, for Your unending mercy, and excessive grace. You cause me to dwell in prosperity as I seek to know Your ways and desire to live a life that proves You are Lord.

In Jesus' Name I pray. Amen.

FACETS

◊   Unfortunately, the words "prosperous" and "prosperity" can have a divisive affect within Christian circles. Why is that so? What does true prosperity mean to you?

◊   Search a concordance or Bible app and jot down the various definitions of how the Bible uses these terms.

DAY 6
I AM GENUINE

"....Anyone who doubts is like a wave in the sea, blown up and down by the wind. Such doubters are thinking two different things at the same time, and they cannot decide about anything they do."
James 1:6b-8a NCV

"But let your 'Yes' be 'Yes,' and your 'No,' 'No.' For whatever is more than these is from the evil one."
Matthew 5:37

"Out of the same mouth proceed blessing and cursing. My brethren, these things ought not to be so. Does a spring send forth fresh water and bitter from the same opening?"
James 3:10-11

"...Do men gather grapes from thorn bushes or figs from thistles? Even so, every good tree bears good fruit, but a bad tree bears bad fruit. A good tree cannot bear bad fruit, nor can a bad tree bear good fruit."
Matthew 7:16b-18

MY PRAYER FOR TODAY:

Dear Heavenly Father,

I wholly desire to be your representative here on this earth and to show forth Your beauty. Lord, Your Word clearly shows that in order to be that representative, I must be singular in my thoughts and purposes. Cause my heart, mind, and mouth to fully agree with Your Word, and to speak only that which comes from faith and confidence in that Word. May I live and act in a way that is not only pleasing to You, but in a way that brings glory to Your name. Help me to press through those times where it may seem more convenient to agree with the majority for the sake of false harmony; help me to take a stand for You especially when it may go against all logic and reason. I want to be a woman who shines bright for You; in whom You find nothing hidden, and nothing to cloud that which would show forth Your light.

Father, in a world that often praises that which You despise, help me to choose Your ways and virtues above those standards that the world holds for itself. You are absolutely true and your ways are sure. Even in those times when I don't understand Your plan, Lord, guide me by your precious Holy Spirit into the ways that lead to eternal reward. Guide my actions and speech in a way that would bring honor to Your Name, not shame. May I be true and pure in my actions and convictions, through each circumstance, both great and small. I thank You, Lord, for lifting me above the fear and opinions of man, and placing my feet on the solid rock of Jesus Christ. May I continue to pursue the imagery and character of Jesus at every opportunity.

In His wonderful Name I pray. Amen.

FACETS

◊   In 2 Timothy 3, Paul describes godlessness in the last days. In verse 5 he writes that there will be people who "have a form of godliness" but deny its power. He contrasts that by reminding Timothy in verse 10 of his own character, and how God miraculously protected him from all sorts of evil. Paul's life was evidence of his faith. What are some ways you display your own "evidence of faith?"

◊   Today, make two lists. On the left, write the word "genuine." To the right, the word "artificial." Go through a thesaurus and list all the synonyms for each word.

DAY 7
I AM PASSIONATE

"As the deer pants for streams of water, so my soul pants for you, O God."
Psalm 42:1

"My soul longs, yes, even faints
For the courts of the Lord;
My heart and my flesh cry out for the living God."
Psalm 84:2

"No, dear brothers and sisters, I am still not all I should be, but I am focusing all my energies on this one thing: Forgetting the past and looking forward to what lies ahead, I strain to reach the end of the race and receive the prize for which God, through Christ Jesus, is calling us up to heaven."
Philippians 3:13-14 NLT

MY PRAYER FOR TODAY:

Dear Heavenly Father,

You created me with dreams and desires. You created me for purposes far above my own comprehension. When I consider these things, I can't help but declare my devotion to You. I am not sluggish or slothful in this amazing life that You have given me. I have every reason to live purposefully, and in a way that is pleasing to You. I am not a lukewarm believer in Christ. I have a testimony that directly points to Jesus and His miraculous work in my life. I have seen Your hand rescue me over and over; I recall those times in my life where You were so evident, that there was no denying Your presence within my circumstances.

I am a woman who lives with passion; who seeks to fulfill all that You've called me to be here on the earth. I am the daughter of a great king whose mission has been determined by her Heavenly Father. The purpose for which I was created must be fulfilled by me, and me alone. I cannot fulfill my destiny without the passion to pursue Jesus at any cost, therefore I declare once again that my life is not my own; that it was purchased by the blood of Jesus on Calvary. This truth in my life energizes me; it gives me every reason to pursue Your high calling on my life. I will continue to be purposeful in my daily living, putting You in your rightful place as first in my life. As I do this, Your fire and Your love will continue to transform me. I want to see Your will done here on earth as it already is in heaven. Help me to take up my role in this life and live each day with passion for You, and for those things which You esteem.

I declare this in faith in Jesus' Name! Amen.

FACETS

◊   What's the difference between being passionate and emotional? How about passionate and dramatic?

◊   What are you truly passionate about?

DAY 8
I AM POWERFUL

"By his divine power, God has given us everything we need for living a godly life. We have received all of this by coming to know him, the one who called us to himself by means of his marvelous glory and excellence."
2 Peter 1:3 NLT

" 'My grace is all you need. My power works best in weakness.' So now I am glad to boast about my weaknesses, so that the power of Christ can work through me."
2 Corinthians 12:9 NLT

"I pray that the eyes of your heart be enlightened in order that you may know the hope to which he has called you, the riches of his glorious inheritance in his people and his incomparably great power for us who believe. That power is the same mighty strength he exerted when he raised Christ from the dead and seated him at the right hand in the heavenly realms, far above all rule and authority, power and dominion, and every name that can be invoked, not only in the present age, but in the age to come."
Ephesians 1:18-21 TNIV

MY PRAYER FOR TODAY:

Dear Heavenly Father,

I confess to You my every weakness. Everything for which I feel inferior or incapable, I give to You. All of my unspoken fears, my insecurities, thoughts of inadequacy and self-deprecating speech, I just simply place before Your feet. You say that when I am weak, then *You* are strong! Oh, Lord, I want my strength to abound from your wellspring of life! Any power that might be displayed through me, Lord, let it be for Your glory, to make Your Name great. May any manifestion of power from my life be a sure sign that You are with me.

May I continually attest to Your work within and throughout my life, displaying to a dying world that true power only comes from a living God. I confess that any resistance to sin, and that the journey toward holiness can only be made by finding my strength in the person of Jesus Christ, and the miraculous working of the Holy Spirit. I willingly yield my heart and mind to believe what You say. You tell me that the power at work in my life is the very same power that raised Jesus from the grave. How incredible is that, Lord! How magnificent is that declaration! Cause these words to stir within me and burst forth when my physical circumstances or my flesh attempt tell me otherwise. I choose to believe that in every moment, whether I feel it or not, you have empowered me with all that I need to live beyond the temporary and physical influences of the world. I am powerful because *You* are mighty in *me*!

I thank you for the evidence, in Jesus' Name. Amen!

FACETS

◊   The word "powerful" probably brings many mental images to your mind. Picture a fierce thunderstorm. How is it that such forceful winds and rain can leave something as delicate as flowers, completely undamaged? What are some interesting images that convey power and tenderness all at once?

◊   In what positive way would you consider yourself powerful?

DAY 9
I AM NOT SHROUDED
IN DARKNESS

"Your Word is a lamp to my feet and a light for my path."
Psalm 119:105

"The spirit of man is the candle of the LORD, searching all the inward parts of the belly."
Proverbs 20:27 KJV

"The LORD's light penetrates the human spirit, exposing every hidden motive."
Proverbs 20:27 NLT

I DECLARE TODAY:

I am the child of the Almighty King and Great God of the universe. He created light and every good and perfect gift is made by His hand. In Him, there is no darkness or shadow of turning. In Him, truth is revealed and darkness cannot hide in His presence. Darkness cannot comprehend Him or His ways. Since I am His child, I am not shrouded in darkness; it cannot overtake me or have its way with me. I am not subject to its dominion or influence because the One who created light dwells within me. Wherever I go, the light of God shines from within and everyone can see this light in me. I am a candle of the Lord; His brightness illuminates who I truly am. I am a new creature in Christ Jesus, and because of that truth, my inner man does not welcome darkness in any form.

Darkness must flee from my presence. It cannot reside within my being or within my household by the authority of Jesus Christ. I refuse to welcome darkness and its subtleties into my life. It is against the character of God; therefore, it must flee from every area of my life.

I declare this in Jesus' mighty Name! Amen.

FACETS

◊   What are some ways in which pop culture attempts to bring darkness into our homes, our children? Consider television programming from 30, 20, and 10 years ago to now (if you can go that far back!).

◊   The influences of the world attempt to desensitize our perception of what is even considered good and evil. How has this cultural campaign increased and strengthened its message over time?

DAY 10

I AM IN FELLOWSHIP WITH THE FATHER

"But he who is joined to the Lord is one spirit with him."
1 Corinthians 6:17

"This one who is life itself was revealed to us, and we have seen him. And now we testify and proclaim to you that he is the one who is eternal life. He was with the Father, and then he was revealed to us. We proclaim to you what we ourselves have actually seen and heard so that you may have fellowship with us. And our fellowship is with the Father and with his Son, Jesus Christ. We are writing these things so that you may fully share our joy."
1 John 1:2-4 NLT

MY PRAYER FOR TODAY:

Heavenly Father,
I thank You that it is Your desire and will for me to commune with You, the God of heaven and earth. How wonderful is your invitation! Through accepting the perfect gift offered by Jesus on the Cross, and by his resurrection to eternal life, You have provided the means to be in fellowship with Your saints, Your church body, and Your Holy Spirit. I am a partaker of your divine nature! I declare Jesus as my Lord and Savior and believe that salvation comes through His Name alone. It is only through the work displayed on the Cross of Calvary that I can boldly proclaim to have fellowship with You.

You have grafted me into Your family, and have provided an inheritance that is beyond my comprehension! I am a joint heir with Christ, and I believe in faith, Father, that I am made righteous in Your eyes through the work of the Cross. How thankful I am for Your provision. No one - no man, not one person – could have done what Jesus did for me. Continue to reveal to me, Father, that I am righteous in your eyes, not by my own works or merit, but because of the free gift You gave to me through Jesus.

I long to fully to walk in the light of Your Word and obey it. I am singular in purpose and in focus, and have no desire to operate in darkness or the works of the flesh. I reject that which would cause distractions and diluted passion toward the things of God in my life. I thank You for ministering angels that surround me; protecting and serving me so that I may continue to pursue all that You have called me to in this life.

I thank You for this supernatural relationship, in Jesus' mighty Name! Amen.

FACETS

◊   Do you have a long-time, yet physically distant friend or family member in your life? If so, when you finally talk or get together, do you feel as if you've never been apart? Jot down the reasons why this is so.

◊   Consider your very best friends – what keeps you close? How do these attributes compare to the ways in which you stay connected to God?

DAY 11

I AM FREE FROM OFFENSE

"It's harder to make amends with an offended friend than to capture a fortified city. Arguments separate friends like a gate locked with iron bars."
Proverbs 18:19 NLT

"And blessed is he who is not offended because of Me."
Matthew 11:6

"Let all bitterness, wrath, anger, clamor, and evil speaking be put away from you, with all malice. And be kind to one another, tenderhearted, forgiving one another, just as God in Christ forgave you."
Ephesians 4:31-32

"Pursue peace with all people, and holiness, without which no one will see the Lord: looking carefully lest anyone fall short of the grace of God; lest any root of bitterness springing up cause trouble, and by this many become defiled..."
Hebrews 12:14-15

MY PRAYER FOR TODAY:

There have been many times in my life where I have felt the sting of another's words. You know them all. There were times when I had experienced serious repercussions based on other people's actions. I have experienced injustice and betrayal. The difference is that now, in my heart, I choose to release everyone who has ever hurt me – physically, emotionally, mentally. I will no longer choose to allow any form of offense to restrict me from being totally free and intimate with You. I will no longer allow any trace of bitterness or resentment to control and burden my heart.

Jesus, You came to release me from the powers of darkness. I will not allow the power of offense to keep me captive. Offense is a work of the evil one, and I choose to live in the light, free from the weight of this deceptive work. In fact, I declare in faith the words of Jesus through Matthew 5:44 working in my life:

"...Love your enemies, bless them that curse you, do good to them that hate you, and pray for them which despitefully use you, and persecute you..."

I choose now to bless every person who has ever hurt me. I ask for Your peace to be upon those who have betrayed my trust. Lord, grant Your merciful lovingkindness to those who have wronged me, and show them Your salvation. I sincerely ask for Your best to be upon them, and to bless them according to Your grace.

Jesus, you died so I could truly live. You came to free my captured heart. How can I live if I am a prisoner to myself? I now choose to look past all offense: real, true, or imagined, that has ever occurred in my life. I choose to fully walk into the light of your goodness and grace. You forgave me of all my past and do not remember my sins when I confess them to You. Who am I to hold on to another's mistakes and bear burdens I was never meant to carry? Thank you, Father, for this gift of forgiveness that allows me to flourish! Amen.

FACETS

◊   The word "offense" in the Bible is the Greek word "scandalon." It literally means the trigger of a set trap. In light of this, how is the spirit of offense like a trap?

◊   What can you do to protect against the dangerous snare of offense while remaining in the love of Christ?

DAY 12
I AM HAND-CRAFTED

"I will praise You, for I am fearfully and wonderfully made;
Marvelous are Your works,
And that my soul knows very well.
My frame was not hidden from You,
When I was made in secret,
And skillfully wrought in the lowest parts of the earth.
Your eyes saw my substance, being yet unformed.
And in Your book they all were written,
The days fashioned for me,
When as yet there were none of them."
Psalm 139:14-16

"Before I formed you in the womb I knew you, before you were
born I set you apart..."
Jeremiah 1:4 (in part)

MY PRAYER FOR TODAY:

Heavenly Father, You are the Creator of all things. I am amazed when I consider the intricacy of life and superior design within everything You have made. I am not an exception to Your works. In fact, I am one of Your most *amazing* works! You created me with such detail, such incredible purpose; who am I to declare otherwise? Although You created all humanity with this marvelous artistry, You made me to be one of a kind. There is no one like me, therefore I am a genuine piece of art! I am a true work of Your hands, a vessel fashioned with love by the most awesome designer.

Forgive me for those times when I have declared anything but Your Word over my life. Forgive me for ever believing the lies of the enemy and succumbing to his fallacies. I believe Your Word above all else, and it declares that "I am fearfully and wonderfully made." I understand that this statement wasn't just for David, but for every person who would dare to believe the truth of that confident profession. I seize this truth for myself today, that I was indeed created by Your hand, and I am authentic and priceless within Your Kingdom. I was created for Your purposes, Lord. All creation points to Your glory and declares your mighty works. May You receive all the praise and glory due Your Name through me. Thank you, Father, for taking such care in Your creation, and for loving me the way You do.

I praise You in Jesus' Name. Amen!

FACETS

◊   Copies of artwork only sell for fractions based on the value of the original piece. If an obscure piece of art by a well-known artist was discovered and put up for sale, what do you expect would happen? What kind of people might be interested in this item?

◊   Give examples of ways in which the world attempts to set value on people. Why does the world's standard make for a faulty foundation?

DAY 13
I AM SALT

"You are the salt of the earth."
Matthew 5:13 (in part)

"Everyone will be salted with fire. Salt is good, but if it loses its saltiness, how can you make it salty again? Have salt in yourselves, and be at peace with each other."
Mark 9:49-50 TNIV

I DECLARE TODAY:

I profess that as Christ's beloved, I am the salt of the earth. The Holy Spirit lives in me and I give Him permission to have His way in me and through me. Because of this, I display the love of God; I have the heart of God; I love what He loves and hate what He hates. His desire for me is that I walk as the salt of the earth – to share Jesus with others in a way that would create a hunger and zeal for the things of the Almighty. When I speak with others, my conversation is salted with flavor and seasoned with grace. I choose my words wisely; I speak good things. Out of my mouth comes encouragement, hope, exhortation, and praise.

As the salt of the earth, I decree Christ's incorruptible nature dwells within me. I am working out my salvation daily in order that I might see more and more of His nature overtake those places in my life that do not reflect the heart and character of God. I want all that God has for me; I want to be all that He has called me to be! I declare that I am seasoned with a zest for life, and a desire to see God's will come to pass here on earth, as it already is in heaven.

I give all glory and honor to You, Lord! In Jesus' Name. Amen.

FACETS

◊ Take a moment to research the properties of salt. What are some ways in which salt is used? In light of Jesus' words, how are we to be like salt?

DAY 14

I AM LIGHT

"You are the light of the world. A city on a hill cannot be hidden. Neither do people light a lamp and put it under a bowl. Instead they put it on its stand, and it gives light to everyone in the house. In the same way, let your light shine before men, that they may see your good deeds and praise your Father in heaven."
Matthew 5:14-16

"For you were once darkness, but now you are light in the Lord. Live as children of light."
Ephesians 5:8

MY PRAYER FOR TODAY:

Dear Heavenly Father,

You reached down from heaven and saved me. You pursued me even when I wanted nothing to do with You. You continued to pour love upon me when I did not yet know You. You saved me from an eternity of separation, an eternity of pain and torment; of suffering and despair. For those reasons alone, it is enough to serve You for the rest of my life. But beyond, that, You have given me a new life here on this earth. You've changed every aspect of living from the day of my salvation. My perspectives are different, my desires are different. You've created me to be a light to others, a vessel filled with Your presence that draws them when they see You in me.

I am no longer shrouded in darkness, and no longer live for myself. I do not stumble about, searching for my own way when trials occur; I have You living inside me, providing constant guidance. Your light in me helps others to find their way to the truth as well. I thank You, Lord, that You are the giver of light; the giver of truth; the giver of true, abundant life. May You continue to have Your way in me, Lord. Help me to recognize Your leading at every turn, remembering that You provide direction in my life, and that I no longer have to make my own way.

I am committed to reading Your Word, and to know it so well, that it pours forth in every situation, in every time of need. I am light to others because Your Word is resident in me and is active in my own life. I thank You, Lord that as You light my way, that same light is providing direction for others in my life.

I declare this in Jesus' Name. Amen.

FACETS

◊   Light can emit softly and delicately, like candle flames. Light can also cut, like laser beams. You wouldn't read in your den with a laser, neither would a surgeon attempt to operate with a lit candlestick! Sometimes a situation calls for us to shine in different ways, based on the need. Note a time when a situation called for you to serve as a "candle," and another time when it was appropriate for you to be more like a "laser."

DAY 15

I AM BOLD

*"In the day when I cried out,
You answered me,
And made me bold with strength in my soul."*
Psalm 138:3

*"The wicked flee when no one pursues,
But the righteous are bold as a lion."*
Proverbs 28:1

*"For God hath not given us the spirit of fear; but of power, and
of love, and of a sound mind."*
2 Timothy 1:7 KJV

MY PRAYER FOR TODAY:

Dear Heavenly Father,

According to Your Word, boldness, when used properly, is a virtue. Boldness is a character trait you desire for me to understand and possess through the Holy Spirit. Help me, Father to use this gift of boldness that You give to your children. May I use this gift in a way that pleases You and brings people to see the beauty and reality of Jesus Christ.

Your Word tells me that You do not give people the spirit of fear, therefore I reject any attempts by the evil one to corrupt my thinking regarding this gift of boldness. Help me to realize that boldness allows me to stand out as the person You created me to be: unique, wonderful, beautiful! You created each of your sons and daughters with a specific personality; with a mixture of talents and abilities that only they possess. You did this so we could shine for You!

Thank You, Father, for helping me step out of my fears and into Your perfect will for my life. I understand that I am to do what You have called me to do, whenever the Holy Spirit leads me. Your Word is full of stories of women who at times, were bold in Your Name. They received Your blessings and changed history because of their ability to step out against the crowd. Cause me to see that this spirit of boldness does not cause me to be the center of attention, but causes YOU to be the center of attention! Let people see You in me because I am led by the Spirit!

In Jesus Name, Amen.

FACETS

◊   Western culture often views boldness as a desirable quality, while other cultures find it rather dishonoring. What is your view on the term "boldness"? When is it appropriate? When would it be completely offensive?

◊   Jesus displayed a holy boldness as he overturned the money changers' tables and vendors' chairs in the temple. (Read Matthew 12:12-17.) How do you think the public majority viewed him and his actions?

◊   Note three other examples in the Bible where people were bold for God.

DAY 16
I AM GIFTED

"I wisdom dwell with prudence, and find out knowledge of witty inventions."
Proverbs 8:12 KJV

"But to each one of us grace has been given as Christ apportioned it. This is why it says: 'When he ascended on high, he led captives in his train and gave gifts to men.' "
Ephesians 4:7-8

MY PRAYER FOR TODAY:

Heavenly Father, when I made a commitment to believe on the Lord Jesus Christ, you immediately gave me a new nature. My entire inner being was transformed the moment I confessed Jesus as my Savior. With that new nature, as I press on to know you better each day, I am discovering Your will and plan for my life. As my Father, You provide all I need in order to be successful in the areas where You have placed me. Therefore, I believe that You gave gifts especially designed to prosper under my stewardship. Forgive me as I have spoken against myself; for times when I have expressed self-loathing and degradation.

Cause me to look beyond my past endeavors to see that You have gifts I have yet to behold! I believe You have equipped me to accomplish all that I am to do. You did not give gifts to Your other children and exclude me. You are lavish in gift-giving and I am learning more about Your generous nature each day. As I discover different facets of Your character, I learn more about who I am in Christ. Your Word states that You've created me in Your image and likeness, so I will believe what You have said. You desire for us, Your children, to reach out beyond ourselves and extend our gifts in order to bring glory to Your Name, in every realm and aspect of life.

As I grow in my knowledge of Christ, my heart yearns for deeper intimacy, allowing You access into every area of my heart. I see You revealing so much more of who I truly am every day. I thank You, God, that You are a gift-giver! You have given me gifts according to my heart's desires, which are actually a reflection of Your desires for me. How amazing! I declare that as I use these talents, I will work in cooperation with You; that I will not seize them and employ them in a corruptible fashion, but I will display Your work through the tools, ideas, creativity, and skills that You have wrought specifically in me. In Jesus' Name I praise You! Amen!

FACETS

◊   Ephesians 4 begins with "As a prisoner for the Lord, then, I urge you to live a life worthy of the calling you have received." The scriptures continue by highlighting that each person has been given grace as Jesus saw fit. What has the Lord graced and gifted you to accomplish? Write down some broad and specific examples.

DAY 17
I AM WISE

"The fear of the LORD is the beginning of knowledge,
But fools despise wisdom and instruction."
Proverbs 1:7

"For the LORD gives wisdom;
From His mouth come knowledge and understanding;
He stores up sound wisdom for the upright;
He is a shield to those who walk uprightly..."
Proverbs 2:6-7

I DECLARE TODAY:

My Heavenly Father holds all wisdom, and it is His desire to grant that wisdom to me. His Word tells me to ask for wisdom, and that I will receive it. God wants me to walk in wisdom and understanding. He does not desire for me to live life on my own, in darkness, apart from the light of His truth. I am wise because my Father finds great joy in granting wisdom to His children. I am wise because I am a hearer and doer of God's Word. I am wise because I give careful attention to God's precepts and commands. His wisdom enables me to walk in submission to His authority, and to those He has put in authority over me.

I am wise because I am a lover of God's Word and His people. I am wise because I do not seek after my own gain; I am more concerned about God receiving the glory in all that I say or do. I am wise because I have chosen to build my life on the solid rock of Jesus Christ; therefore I cannot be shaken. I am wise because I heed the instruction and rebuke of my elders in the faith. I am wise because I give thought to my actions and examine the motivations of my heart. I am wise because I have chosen to give God the first fruits of all my increase. I am wise because I trust my Heavenly Father, even when I cannot see or comprehend His ways and methods.

I am grateful for all that God has done in order for me to gain His heavenly insight. It pleased Him to give up His only Son on the Cross in order that I might be reconciled into a right relationship with the One who created me and knew me before I came into being. I attribute any success I may have in this life to the One who has granted me wisdom.

I declare this in Jesus' Name. Amen.

FACETS

◊   The Lord looks favorably to those who search for widsom and understanding. Consider young King Solomon. (Read 1 Kings 3:1-15.) What stands out to you in this story?

◊   Reflect on a situation where God provided you with supernatuaral wisdom, either to help someone in need, or provided you much needed personal clarity.

DAY 18
I AM ABLE

"Not that we are competent in ourselves to claim anything for ourselves, but our competence comes from God. He has made us competent as ministers of a new covenant—not of the letter but of the Spirit; for the letter kills, but the Spirit gives life."
2 Corinthians 3:5-6

"And God is able to make all grace abound to you, so that in all things at all times, having all that you need, you will abound in every good work."
2 Corinthians 9:8

MY PRAYER FOR TODAY:

Lord of Heaven, You live inside of me. Your entire love story written to mankind is all about a God who loved imperfect people. You loved imperfect people so much, You sent Your only perfect Son to die on our behalf, so You could dwell within the hearts of humanity. Your ways are astounding; Your love, outrageous. Heavenly Father, I ask that You would continue to remind me of this perfect love during times of weakness; during those moments that try to overtake me, when I hear the voice of the enemy who tells me that I can't accomplish what You've put in my heart. Lord, because of You, I am able. Only because of what You have done, and because of who You are, I can trust You with all that I am.

I am able to accomplish what You require of me. I am able to hear Your voice; I am able to discern truth and wield the sword of the Spirit in a way that causes the enemy to flee. I am able to love beyond any natural capacity because You have taken residence within me and cause me to be an extension of Yourself, especially to those who hurt and mistreat me. I am able to let go of offenses; I am able to forgive because of Your forgiveness. I am able to dispense joy to others because of the joy I have found in You. I'm completely able to walk in peace, not confusion; to rely upon Your wisdom and not my own carnal knowledge. I am able to bring solutions to difficult situations because I'm relying on your Holy Spirit to speak through me. Lord, because of You, I'm completely capable.

Continue to reveal the great ability I have through Your Spirit, Lord. Thank You for showing me that I have overcome all obstacles because Jesus has overcome the world. You are my greatest encourager; my best friend. It amazes me that You, the King of the universe, believes in me. What can I not do through You?

Have Your way, Lord. In Jesus' Name, Amen.

FACETS

◊   Has anyone ever told you, or have you ever told *yourself* that you weren't capable of _____? (Fill in the blank.) Did that statement or belief cloud your thinking regarding your abilities? Look back on your notes from Day 16. Do you see any correlation between your giftings and how you might currently view your ability?

DAY 19
I AM A WOMAN OF INFLUENCE

"For whoso findeth me findeth life, and shall obtain favour of the LORD."
Proverbs 8:35 KJV

"Charm is deceitful, and beauty is vain, but a woman who fears the LORD is to be praised. Give her of the fruit of her hands, and let her works praise her in the gates."
Proverbs 31:30-31 ESV

I DECLARE TODAY:

      As the daughter of the Only True and Heavenly King, I am a woman destined to be a partaker of His divine nature. As my God has empowered me to live uprightly through His Holy Spirit, and as I choose to work out my salvation in godly fear, I am designed to be a woman of great influence. As God's character and nature is displayed through me, I draw others to seek the face of God. My character becomes more like my Father's every day. As I become the woman that He has seen before the foundations of the earth were created, He is pleased that I am growing and changing, becoming more like Him as I understand His goodness and grace. He finds pleasure as my influence attracts people to pursue intimacy with the Lover of their souls.

      My influence wields amazing authority. Through the empowerment of the Holy Spirit, I choose to use this influence in order to bring others into a deeper relationship with my Heavenly Father. It is my privilege to draw others to God as I display His love and character toward them. I am a woman of influence simply by being one who hungers and thirsts for God's righteousness. I don't have to try; I don't have to demand or command through my own personal efforts. I am a woman of influence because God's Spirit dwells within me and I give Him first place in my heart in order that all may see Him through me.

      I declare this in faith, in Jesus' Name! Amen.

FACETS

◊   List some of the ways in which the world's definition of an "influential woman" differs with how God pictures her. What are the most striking contrasts?

◊   Describe one influential woman who has been a part of your life. What do you admire most about her?

DAY 20
I AM FORGIVEN

"Then Jesus said to her, 'Your sins are forgiven.' "
Luke 7:47

"But now in Christ Jesus you who once were far off have been brought near by the blood of Christ."
Ephesians 2:13

"Blessed is he whose transgression is forgiven,
Whose sin is covered."
Psalm 32:1

MY PRAYER FOR TODAY:

Dear Heavenly Father,

I was once separated from You, from Your holiness and perfection. I once lived for myself and did not recognize or understand the depth of love displayed to me when Jesus willingly died on the Cross for my sins. When I lived for myself, my first priority was my needs, my wants, and my desires. But by Your mercy, Lord, You drew me to Yourself and sought me when I wasn't even searching for You. Thank You, Lord, for pursuing me when I was blind and deaf to this amazing love. Thank You for opening my eyes, ears, and heart to Your Spirit, and for forgiving me of everything I have done that was against Your ways. How grateful I am for complete forgiveness of all my sins.

I thank You that I can stand boldly, confidently, and freely before You, just as a child would come to her father. You are my Father, my Creator and Redeemer, and I stand before You today with a heart full of gratitude that there is nothing between us that would separate me from Your presence. Your forgiveness is full and complete, and I embrace that forgiveness and purpose to walk in it today, knowing that I am wholly and extravagantly loved by You.

I declare this today, in Jesus' Name. Amen!

FACETS

◊   D.L. Moody once said, "Forgiveness is not that stripe which says, 'I will forgive, but not forget.' It is not to bury the hatchet with the handle sticking out of the ground, so you can grasp it the minute you want it." Micah 7:19 says that the Lord will cast all our sins into the depths of the sea, and to paraphrase Psalm 103:12, God has cast away our sins as far is the east from the west. If our Lord has forgiven and forgotten our trespasses so completely, can we say the same for ourselves?

◊   Note that moment when you realized God's forgiveness was for *you*. Perhaps you encountered the Lord's forgiveness years ago, or maybe *today* is the day. Please write a short poem or song describing that moment, or one conveying your thanks or thoughts toward Him.

DAY 21
I AM A NEW CREATION

"...I tell you the truth, no one can see the kingdom of God unless he is born again."
John 3:3

"...if anyone is in Christ, he is a new creation; the old has gone, the new has come!"
2 Corinthians 5:17

MY PRAYER FOR TODAY:

Dear Heavenly Father,

I thank you that Your Word declares that I am fearfully and wonderfully made. Although we continue to live upon the earth that awaits complete restoration and renewal from sin and death, You have given mankind the opportunity to become new and completely whole in spirit. I am grateful for the eyes of faith that come with a renewed spirit in Christ Jesus, helping me to see that I truly am a new creation. No longer am I bound to the things of the world; I am not a slave to unrighteousness.

Evil does not rule my mind, emotions, or my heart. When I believed upon the Lord Jesus Christ for my salvation, my inner being completely changed. You transform me from the inside out! Lord, help me to continue to work out my salvation according to Philippians 2:12. Help me to continually see that you never do things "half way," therefore, I declare in Jesus' Name that Your work in me is not in vain. I am grateful for this new life! Amen.

FACETS

◊   Through Christ's blood, we didn't just receive a makeover--we got a complete rebuild! Our inner man became alive, and our hearts were made anew. Ezekiel 36:26 prophesies to Israel, *"I will give you a new heart and put a new spirit within you; I will take the heart of stone out of your flesh and give you a new heart of flesh."* Because we are also heirs of the blessings of Abraham, this promise is for us, too.

◊   Although God is responsible for the 'heart transplant,' we must renew our mind to match that new heart with the Word of God. Consider your thought life. What needs to change in order to match what God's Word says? For example, if you are plagued with worry, jot it down, and then beside it write out the scripture that deals with that issue, like Matthew 6:25.

DAY 22
I AM NOT FORGOTTEN

"The LORD himself goes before you and will be with you; he will never leave you nor forsake you. Do not be afraid; do not be discouraged."
Deuteronomy 31:8

"For the eyes of the LORD range throughout the earth to strengthen those whose hearts are fully committed to him."
2 Chronicles 16:9

"Then those who feared the LORD talked with each other, and the LORD listened and heard. A scroll of remembrance was written in his presence concerning those who feared the LORD and honored his name."
Malachi 3:16

MY PRAYER FOR TODAY:

Heavenly Father, Your eyes are on the sparrow; You say not one of them falls to the ground without your knowledge. You know the numbers of hairs on my head. If You are mindful of even the birds, then how much more, Lord, are You truly mindful of me? Your Word says You are familiar with all my ways, and You will perfect that which concerns me.

The Bible is Your love letter written to me, Lord. All throughout its pages, You speak of Your concern, Your care, Your complete awareness of my comings and goings. How could I remain in a place where I feel as if no one cared about me? Even if it were true, Lord, and not one person exhibited concern for me, I know You do. You have not forgotten me, nor will You ever forget me. I'm here to execute Your will for my life, and I will not allow the evil one to misalign my thoughts with his. I will continue to choose to bring my thoughts into proper alignment with Your Word.

Teach me, Father, to desire Your approval, and Yours alone. Instruct me in finding the highest value knowing I've done my best for You. Show me to truly be content with Your affirmation, and not that which comes from man. I ask that You continue to inspire me; that I be not driven to receive accolades from people, but that I would wholly strive to please You in all that I do, and in all that I say. Help me, Lord, to acknowledge others when I'm overlooked; help me to serve out of compassion and not out of a fleshly desire for man's reward. Lord, I look to You; I long to serve You well and for You to take delight in my service.

In those moments when I feel forgotten, remind me, Lord, that You see and know all things. You take great pleasure when I serve, give, love, and listen with a heart that desires only Your approval. Help me to continually crucify the flesh so that I may be motivated by Your pleasure alone, in Jesus' Name. Amen.

FACETS

◊   Do you remember participating in fire drills when you were a child? A plan of action was created and executed to ensure safety in the event of an actual emergency. Our thought life is crucial to our spiritual growth, and must continually be guarded. The enemy constantly attempts to trick us into wrong thinking, especially about our personal value - to others and to God Himself. Today, write out a plan of action to escape the enemy when he comes to try and trap your thinking. What can you do to remain free of the enemy's snare when he tries to enter your thought life?

DAY 23
I AM SET APART

"Consecrate yourselves therefore, and be holy, for I am the Lord your God. 'And you shall keep My statutes, and perform them: I am the Lord who sanctifies you.' "
Leviticus 20:7-8

"Know that the LORD has set apart the godly for himself; the LORD will hear when I call to him."
Psalm 4:3

"Once you were alienated from God and were enemies in your minds because of your evil behavior. But now he has reconciled you by Christ's physical body through death to present you holy in his sight, without blemish and free from accusation..."
Colossians 1:21-22

I DECLARE TODAY:

I am a woman who has been reserved by God Himself, by my Heavenly Father, for His pleasure and divine plans. I find great joy in knowing that I am His. My God and King has set me apart from corruption and decay – from the things of the world that produce death and have no place in Him. I am a vessel that pours forth life and purity. I believe that He has saved me from an eternity of separation in the life to come, and that He also saved me in order for His plans to be carried out here on earth. Like fine crystal, I am set apart for special purposes. Yet I am not simply "on display;" I am active in pursuing what God has called me to in this life.

His treasury is filled with unique and beautiful vessels. I am in awe when I consider that He has chosen me and has called me His very own. I understand that as I am set apart, sanctified and called holy for my Heavenly Father's purposes, that great responsibility rests upon me. I realize I am responsible to reflect my Father's love to others; that His anointing is costly and is to be considered with great reverence. I am not set apart in order to point out others' faults or to think myself more highly than I ought; on the contrary, I am set apart to display and activate the love of Jesus in every situation I encounter.

Help me, Lord, to understand in a greater way, how to walk a sanctified life, daily in Your presence. There is no greater calling than that which enables me to live this life of purity and holiness. I thank You, Lord, for setting me apart; for reserving me and preserving me. May Your will for my life be done on earth as it already is in heaven!

In Jesus' Name. Amen.

FACETS

◊   Many couples receive chinaware as a wedding gift, and use it only for special occasions. Women wear elegant gowns the day they say, "I do." It would be rare for people to eat on china everyday, and downright weird if a bride wore her wedding dress as casual wear! What parallels can you draw from this illustration to your life as being set apart by God?

DAY 24

I AM CLEAN

"Purge me with hyssop, and I shall be clean;
Wash me, and I shall be whiter than snow."
Psalm 51:7

"Now a leper came to Him, imploring Him, kneeling down
to Him and saying to Him, 'If You are willing, You can make
me clean.' Then Jesus, moved with compassion, stretched out
His hand and touched him, and said to him, 'I am willing; be
cleansed.' "
Mark 1:40-41

"You are already clean because of the word which I have
spoken to you."
John 15:3

MY PRAYER FOR TODAY:

Dear Heavenly Father,

How grateful I am for the washing of the Word in my life! How amazing it is to know that Jesus' perfect sacrifice caused the spiritual veil to forever be torn in two, granting me access to the King of heaven and earth and the Lover of my soul!

Lord, I thank You for the gift of repentance; for the ability to come before You during every season of my life. Your goodness and mercy draw me to You, even in my most wretched state. Thank You for Your unending pursuit of me! I cannot bear the thought of a lifetime of separation from You, from the One who loves me more than I can imagine.

When I go astray, or when I simply choose to ignore Your goodness, how grateful I am for this love that constantly yearns for me! You bring me back to you. You melt my heart when it is cold and hard. You break down the walls I erect there; the walls I create when I choose to live outside of Your protection. Oh Lord, how great is Your kindness and how deep is Your understanding.

Father, continue to lead me by Your hand, just as a good and loving father would do with his little child. Your love is my life, Your truth is my lifeline, Your life is my heart's desire. I want to be with You forever. Thank You for cleansing me through and through.

In Jesus' Name I pray. Amen.

FACETS

◊   There are several words in the Bible that are translated as "clean." All convey a sense of purity, either morally, physically, or spiritually. Jesus admonished the Pharisees in Matthew 23:24-28 and Luke 11:39, 40 regarding outward behavior and appearances and to be clean from within. Cleanness, according to the Bible, conveys the absence of mixture of both the Word of God and the condition of our own hearts.

◊   Find the word "clean" in several verses in both the Old and New Testaments. Write down several scriptures that highlight this concept. Write your personal observations of each scripture.

DAY 25
I AM REDEEMED

"But thanks be to God that, though you used to be slaves to sin, you have come to obey from your heart the pattern of teaching that has now claimed your allegiance. You have been set free from sin and have become slaves to righteousness."
Romans 6:17-18

"Christ redeemed us from the curse of the law by becoming a curse for us, for it is written: 'Cursed is everyone who is hung on a tree.' He redeemed us in order that the blessing given to Abraham might come to the Gentiles through Christ Jesus, so that by faith we might receive the promise of the Spirit."
Galatians 3:13-14

"And they sang a new song, saying:
`You are worthy to take the scroll,
And to open its seals;
For You were slain,
And have redeemed us to God by Your blood
Out of every tribe and tongue and people and nation,
And have made us kings and priests to our God;
And we shall reign on the earth.' "
Revelation 5:9-10

MY PRAYER FOR TODAY:

Dear Heavenly Father,

When I consider the price Jesus paid so that I might not be separated from You, I am overwhelmed. What can I do or say that would ever communicate my thanks to the One who loves me more than I can fathom? What would be appropriate, other than to offer my life to the One who gave it to me? Help me to understand what it means according to Acts 17:28, to truly live, move, and have my being in You, Lord. Help me to understand what it means to be a slave to righteousness, and that there, in that position, is where true freedom is found.

What Jesus endured in order to bring me out of darkness, out of an unclean life, is more than anyone can imagine. How deep is Your love for me, God! How unsearchable are the depths of that love! May I spend my days here on earth considering the cost of my redemption and the power of the blood that purchased me. May I be a bondservant of Christ, pointing everyone to true freedom that can only be found in You.

In Jesus' Name I pray. Amen.

FACETS

◊   Modern society does not readily lend itself to understanding the concept or power of the word 'redemption.' Jesus was born during a time where physical captivity was a normal component of society. The slave market was a thriving enterprise at that time. Slaves were looked upon as property, and the idea of human rights did not apply. All rights and freedoms were stripped once a soul entered this miserable existence.

◊   Do a quick study on slavery in the Roman era. Describe how completely Jesus set us free of bondage in light of your findings.

*For excellent reading on this subject, read Rick Renner's book, "Dressed to Kill."

DAY 26
I AM NOT FATHERLESS

"Sing to God, sing praise to his name,
extol him who rides on the clouds—
his name is the LORD—
and rejoice before him.
A father to the fatherless, a defender of widows,
is God in his holy dwelling.
God sets the lonely in families,
he leads forth the prisoners with singing;
but the rebellious live in a sun-scorched land."
Psalm 68:4-6

"And because we are his children, God has sent the Spirit
of his Son into our hearts, prompting us to call out, 'Abba,
Father.' "
Galatians 4:6 NLT

MY PRAYER FOR TODAY:

My true home is in heaven. My life is found in You, and in You alone. You are everything to me. I desire to be a reflection of You here on this earth, until I am with You for all eternity. I understand through Your Word, and by revelation through the Holy Spirit that You are my true Father. You are the example for every earthly father, and although earthly fathers may not act or love like You do, *You* are the one and only rightful example of fatherhood.

I make a decision now to see You in this light — as my Father — One who is good and loving; One who defends and protects His children; One who listens and laughs and finds joy in the little things I do; the One who encourages me and helps me navigate through difficult trials. You are the Father who disciplines in love, for the right reasons. You are the Father who demonstrates unending patience and kindness. I know you as my Father who lavishes me with the most incredible gift: the gift of Jesus Christ. You loved me so much, that You gave Your only Son for me as a ransom that I might be brought back into relationship with You, reconciled to You by Jesus' precious blood. You saved me from an eternity of separation from You, and from an earthly life filled with only temporal things. You wanted me so much that You were willing to give up your perfect Son, so that I could experience the fullness of Your joy here on earth, and in the life to come. I thank You, for I not only call You my King and my God, but Your desire is for me to know You as Father, my daddy! Hallelujah! I praise You for being so incredibly good and faithful. I can always count on You. When I call, You are there. Before I even whisper Your Name, You are present, comforting me, embracing me the way only You can.

Thank You, Father, for revealing this truth to me. May I never forget to see You this way. In Jesus' beautiful Name, Amen!

FACETS

63% of youth suicides are from fatherless homes
(U.S. Dept. of Health and Human Services, Bureau of the Census)

71% of high school drop-outs are from fatherless homes
(National Principals Association Report on the state of high schools)

85% of all youths in prison today are from fatherless homes
(U.S. Dept. of Justice)

85% of all children that exhibit behavioral disorders
come from fatherless homes
(United States Center for Disease Control)

Malachi 4 prophesies that before the Lord's return, He will send (the spirit of) Elijah and that he "shall turn the heart of the fathers to the children, and the heart of the children to their fathers…" We must find encouragement and comfort in these words, knowing that God will fulfill His desire within the hearts of men.

◊ Growing up, who was your paternal figure? Can you highlight some experiences that led to the way you see the role of a father in the home today?

◊ What are some qualities that you directly identify in a masculine or paternal way? List them on your page.

◊ Today, please pray for those who are fatherless and hurting.

DAY 27

I AM SPIRIT-DRIVEN

"For they that are after the flesh do mind the things of the flesh; but they that are after the Spirit the things of the Spirit."
Romans 8:5 KJV

"For all who are led by the Spirit of God are children of God."
Romans 8:14 NLT

MY PRAYER FOR TODAY:

Father, I thank You for the divine nature You placed within me when I received Jesus Christ as my Lord and Savior. Without this new nature, I would be powerless to diligently seek out and comprehend the treasures hidden within Your Word. I would be utterly incapable to minister truth to others in a way that would impact eternity. Your Holy Spirit lives within me; therefore, I am empowered to carry out your desires for my life. You created me in your image and likeness. My inner being – my spirit – has been transformed by your gift of salvation.

I choose to continually run to the Cross; to the place of mercy and grace, to be a dispenser of that grace that was so generously given to me. I reject the distractions of the enemy and the worthlessness of seeking after carnal desires. You enable me to properly discern Your Word and to hear your voice. I will not manipulate Your Yord for personal or temporal gain. I will not abuse this costly gift of liberty by using it inappropriately. I pray, Father, that You would find me blameless and upright in my desire to hear Your voice. You are my reward, and I am pursuing You with a pure heart. Prepare me, Lord; cause me to be a hearer and doer of Your Word to an even greater degree so that You may touch others through me. I choose to mind the things of the Spirit in order to know You in a deeper way. I long to see Your mighty hand of wonder working miracles upon the earth. I desire to be the daughter through which you may work unhindered, for such a time as this.

I pray this in the precious Name of Jesus. Amen.

FACETS

◊　Make two columns on today's journal page, one titled "Flesh," and the other, "Spirit." Find all the scripture references you can and list characteristics in the appropriate columns.

◊　Now picture a balance scale. With your written list, mentally place the characteristics that currently relate to your personal life on the appropriate side. Which way is the balance leaning?

DAY 28
I AM GOD'S TEMPLE

"Do you not know that you are the temple of God and that the Spirit of God dwells in you?"
1 Corinthians 3:16 KJV

"Or do you not know that your body is the temple of the Holy Spirit who is in you, whom you have from God, and you are not your own?"
1 Corinthians 6:19 NLT

I DECLARE TODAY:

It pleases my God and Father to dwell not only with me, but in me. His desire for me is magnified through the truth of His Word, which repeatedly declares His yearning for an abode within the heart of one who loves Him. As God's chosen vessel, it pleases me to show Him the honor He greatly deserves by living a life of purity and truth. I am called to love what He loves, and to hate what He hates. Therefore, I choose to love wisdom, knowledge and understanding. I choose to love even when I am persecuted and mistreated by others. I choose to walk in such a way that is upright, in which my God and King finds great delight.

I am God's temple of holiness. I desire to live undefiled through making personal choices that display I am consecrated to the One who loves me beyond description. As my body is His chosen dwelling place, it is my desire to hear from my Father through His Word, and to act in obedience according to what is written. I find His commandments are not burdensome; they are life to me. I declare that as a daughter of the Almighty King, I am separated, holy, and preserved for His good pleasure. I am the daughter of a good and gracious God, and He is not a man that He should lie. My Heavenly Father's character is displayed through Jesus, who embodied God in the flesh. His perfect love for me demands that I be transformed into His image and likeness by the renewing of my mind. Therefore, I declare that as God's holy temple, I am a woman set apart for purity, power, and purpose.

I declare this in Jesus' Name. Amen.

FACETS

◊   Picture the exterior of your home at the peak of perfection. Imagine your finely detailed, manicured lawn; the flawless paint job: lighting and fixtures to highlight its beauty. (Picture it however you want, just see it as completely stunning!) Now imagine you walk into the living room and find that it's an absolute wreck! Would this be acceptable to you? How are we to treat our physical bodies, as they are now vessels purposed for the work of the Lord?

◊   Are there any areas that might need special treatment? For instance, if you're a night-owl and REALLY don't get enough sleep, could you agree to shaving a little bit of time from your evening to get some much needed rest? List anything you can think of on today's journal page.

DAY 29
I AM WHOLE

"Then great multitudes came to Him, having with them the lame, blind, mute, maimed, and many others; and they laid them down at Jesus' feet, and He healed them. So the multitude marveled when they saw the mute speaking, the maimed made whole, the lame walking, and the blind seeing; and they glorified the God of Israel."
Matthew 15:30-31 NKJV

"And he said unto her, 'Daughter, thy faith hath made thee whole; go in peace, and be whole of thy plague.' "
Mark 5:34 KJV

"Grace and peace be multiplied to you in the knowledge of God and of Jesus our Lord, as His divine power has given to us all things that pertain to life and godliness, through the knowledge of Him who called us by glory and virtue, by which have been given to us exceedingly great and precious promises, that through these you may be partakers of the divine nature, having escaped the corruption that is in the world through lust."
2 Peter 1:2-4

MY PRAYER FOR TODAY:

Lord, You are more than capable of bringing about my healing and wholeness through Your Word, and through Jesus Christ, to whom I pledge my life. In fact, Lord, through the precious gift of salvation, You have already provided wholeness within my inner being, the true "me" - my spirit nature. When I confessed Jesus as Lord and accepted Your gift of eternal salvation, it was then that you provided me with all I need in order to live a godly, just, and pleasing life.

I ask, Heavenly Father, that You would daily show me how to access Your promises and make it evident, Lord, that You have indeed given me all these things. Your righteousness is already mine! Your victory is already mine! Your gift of healing is already mine! You are not a "half way" God; not a "just enough" God. You are the God who sees the end from the beginning, and You are an extreme provider. It is not Your nature to give incomplete gifts. There is no half way or average provision within Your Word!

I thank You, God, that You are opening my eyes to the fullness of Your promises provided with the gift of salvation. I ask for forgiveness, Lord, for ever thinking that perhaps You were hiding provision from within my reach. I profess now, Lord, that You gave me all that was required to live successfully on this earth. Through the blood of Jesus, You not only provided what is necessary to live eternally; when You offered Your Son on the Cross, You gave every good and perfect gift to me. I declare today that through salvation in Christ, I am whole; there is nothing missing from Your promises, and there is nothing broken in me. Help me to grasp this truth in the physical realm, in this natural state of being in which I live. I desire the supernatural to supersede the natural in my life! I long to live out the life Jesus came to give me – one that is abundant and blessed!

I thank You for it today, in Jesus' Name. Amen!

◊   Read the accounts of four very important women in the gospels: Matthew 9:20-22; Matthew 26:6-13; John 4:7-30, and John 8:1-11. Reflect on their stories and how Jesus impacted them. What of each of these women's stories stands out to you most?

DAY 30
I AM HEALED

"Surely He has borne our griefs
And carried our sorrows;
Yet we esteemed Him stricken,
Smitten by God, and afflicted.
But He was wounded for our transgressions,
He was bruised for our iniquities;
The chastisement for our peace was upon Him,
And by His stripes we are healed."
Isaiah 53:4-5

"Our Father in heaven, hallowed be your name, your kingdom
come, your will be done on earth as it is in heaven."
Matthew 6:9-10 TNIV

"Woman, you are set free from your infirmity."
Luke 13:12

MY PRAYER FOR TODAY:

Dear Heavenly Father, I thank You for the gift of life and healing that flows from the finished work of the Cross. Jesus paid the penalty of sin and reclaimed all authority and power which was subdued from Adam at the dawn of creation. Your gift of salvation includes wholeness in my body, soul, and spirit. Nothing can withstand the power of Jesus' blood as I grasp Your Word and firmly believe healing became mine when the Lord Jesus took captivity captive. I believe that I rule and reign with Christ, that Satan is under my feet because I stand firmly on the Rock, Jesus. He is my sure foundation, and I will not be moved. I will take hold of what I cannot see; I will align my thoughts and my words to confess Your good promises and I absolutely reject the enemy's lies and attempt to sway me from my ruling position within Your kingdom.

I call out Satan and his plans to divide, deride, and desecrate that which is no longer his. I am the daughter of the Most High Living God, the Lord of Glory, and in my Lord there is no sickness, disease, no manner of mental anxiety, no fear, no dread. I thank You, Father, for this is how You see me: a woman fully restored, healed from all manner of sickness, and fully capable to minister in ways which You have prescribed for me. Cause me to see as You see, Lord. Align my own words and my heart to Your truth. Dispatch Your ministering angels as I allow Your peace to wash over me. Your words are sure, Your promises are solid. You are faithful to carry out all Your plans concerning my future. I am a woman set free, and I boldly proclaim this truth by the power released through the shed blood of Jesus. In His Name I pray, Amen!

FACETS

◊   To paraphrase Revelation 12:11, it says that the saints of God overcame the enemy by the blood of the Lamb and the word of their testimony. Our testimony is a blow to the kingdom of darkness. Satan hates it when God's people declare victory. Have you ever received a miraculous healing, or prayed for someone who received healing? Record a testimony of that miracle moment here.

◊   If you have not yet witnessed or received healing for which you are praying and standing firm, stay encouraged by yesterday's Facet. Write your prayer of thanks for a manifestation of this healing and continue to hold fast to your confession of faith!

DAY 31
I AM A PEACEMAKER

"Great peace have they who love your law, and nothing can make them stumble."
Psalm 119:165

"The wise woman builds her house, but with her own hands the foolish one tears hers down."
Proverbs 14:1

"Peace I leave with you, my peace I give unto you: not as the world giveth, give I unto you.
Let not your heart be troubled, neither let it be afraid."
John 14:27 KJV

I DECLARE TODAY:

I am not a foolish woman who plucks down her own household with her hands. Because I am a new creature in Christ Jesus and I have been made alive unto God, I no longer work against His kingdom authority or His ways. I am no longer a blind agent to dark conspiracies or deception. I am not a woman who uses manipulation for increase; I am neither rebellious nor contentious, therefore, Satan has no legal access into my life. My love for people has been made pure through the washing of God's Word and through my application of the Word in my life, where in times past Satan had the ability to corrupt my desires for friendship or for gain of false peace through my ignorance and carnal nature.

As the daughter of the One and Only True King, I am anointed to administer truth in love through godly fear. It is my heavenly mandate that I operate in the ministry imparted to me, that being the ministry of reconciliation unto God. It is my duty and obligation to live in such a way that would promote true restoration on any level: within my family, my friendships, and my family members within the faith. No one is exempt from benefiting in this ministry that has been granted to me by my Heavenly Father. I am called to bring and make peace in any situation of which I am apart; I am called to live at peace with everyone with whom I interact, regardless of the level of involvement. I thank You God, for anointing me to be a peacemaker, allowing me to work hand in hand with You for Your divine and eternal purposes.

In Jesus' Name. Amen.

FACETS

◊   What are the differences between someone who might act to "preserve" peace rather than to "make" peace?

◊   We have all at various times, chosen to act as the peacekeeper. Recall one of those instances and reflect on why you chose that response.

◊   Can you think of how you might serve as a peacemaker in a current situation? Share your thoughts here.

DAY 32

I AM A WARRIOR

" 'Do not be afraid or discouraged because of this vast army.
For the battle is not yours, but God's.' "
2 Chronicles 20:15

"Now when He was asked by the Pharisees when the kingdom
of God would come, He answered them and said, 'The
kingdom of God does not come with observation; nor will they
say, "See here!" or "See there!" 'For indeed, the kingdom of
God is within you.' "
Luke 17:20-21

"For though we walk in the flesh, we do not war according to
the flesh. For the weapons of our warfare are not carnal but
mighty in God for pulling down strongholds, casting down
arguments and every high thing that exalts itself against the
knowledge of God, bringing every thought into captivity to the
obedience of Christ, and being ready to punish all disobedience
when your obedience is fulfilled."
2 Corinthians 10:3-6

"Put on the whole armor of God, that you may be able to stand
against the wiles of the devil. For we do not wrestle against
flesh and blood, but against principalities, against powers,
against the rulers of the darkness of this age, against spiritual
hosts of wickedness in the heavenly places."
Ephesians 6:11-18

MY PRAYER FOR TODAY:

You are not only my Heavenly Father; You are my King. You are Commander over the greatest warriors the world has ever known. Throughout time, You have led countless men and women to battle in the spirit, winning wars imperceptible to the human eye. Your command continues through this day, and I am fully equipped to engage the enemy now through Your powerful Word.

While He was on the earth, Jesus said that the kingdom of heaven was at hand, and that the kingdom of heaven was within. I am fully pursuaded, Lord, that not only do You rule as a righteous King on high, but within the very center of my being. Your kingdom IS here, in me. You are daily training me to fight spiritual battles through the Holy Spirit and your Living Word. I am clothed with the armor of God, therefore serve as a threat to the enemy. I am not simply a defensive soldier; I am an offensive one as well, thwarting Satan's attempts at destruction ahead of time. Through wisdom, discernment, and putting into practice what I understand from Your Word, I cannot be deceived by the schemes of the enemy. I confess that my battles are your battles. I give up any right to call them my own, for You promise to be with me always. You fight on my behalf, yet You cause me to wage war in the supernatural using Your Word and the love of Christ that has been shed throughout my heart. Just as the Israelites had to physically overcome enemies in order take hold of the promised land, I believe You have equipped me in order to rightfully possess what is mine in the spiritual realm. Trust in Your Word surely brings about victory, and for that I rejoice, even before I see the results.

I continue to press on through Jesus' Name. Amen.

FACETS

◊   Paul often used military metaphors and analogies to illustrate biblical principles in his letters to the churches. His examples would have been well understood, for the people of that period would have been acquainted with various aspects of military life. Take some time to research military training methods of the ancient Roman army, and write down any personal revelations.

DAY 33
I AM MORE THAN
A CONQUEROR

"But thanks be to God, which giveth us the victory through our Lord Jesus Christ."
1 Corinthians 15:57 KJV

"For whatever is born of God overcomes the world. And this is the victory that has overcome the world--our faith. Who is he who overcomes the world, but he who believes that Jesus is the Son of God?"
1 John 5:4-5

MY PRAYER FOR TODAY:

Father, You have planted within me seeds of greatness. I have unlimited access to the victory You have given me through Jesus Christ, my Savior. Because He lives, I live a new life. I am not bound and captive to what is now in my past. Before Christ came to give me true life, I had no idea I walked like one who was already dead: dead in sin and dead in works. Help me to perceive and truly understand, Lord, the victory that Christ came to give me personally. Let it manifest throughout all my days on this earth. Allow me to perceive daily that I walk in victory over the flesh, over my old ways of thinking, and attempts at self-preservation. I willingly give my whole heart to You, Lord.

What can I possibly reserve within myself that would create a difference for eternity? Without the revelation of the true victory I hold within Christ, I can give nothing to those in need; I can do or say nothing that holds eternal value. I recognize that the fruit of my lips can only produce life when I understand that you have given me victory to overcome every evil on the earth. I acknowledge that my thoughts outside of Yours do not create any value within the eternal realm.

Without Your Holy Spirit guiding me, giving me purpose, harnessing that which is corruptible within me, I cannot perceive Your greatness, or the greatness You have purposed for me. Therefore, I speak over my life, over my thoughts, and over my actions that I will continually come into alignment with Your divine Word, that I will grasp more fully each day what it truly means to live victoriously in Christ Jesus.

Let Your will be done in my life according to Your Word, in Jesus' Name. Amen.

FACETS

◊   Read Joshua 7 and 8. Why were the Israelites defeated the first time they attacked Ai?

◊   What did God say to Joshua in 8:2 regarding victory? What in this verse shows that the Israelites were destined to be more than conquerors in this battle?

◊   What was the difference between the aftermath of the battle of Jericho (Joshua 6:24) and this second battle at Ai?

DAY 34
I AM CHOSEN

"You did not choose Me, but I chose you and appointed you that you should go and bear fruit, and that your fruit should remain, that whatever you ask the Father in My name He may give you."
John 15:16

"God picked you out as his from the very start. Think of it: included in God's original plan of salvation by the bond of faith in the living truth."
2 Thessalonians 2:13 The Message

"But you are a chosen generation, a royal priesthood, a holy nation, His own special people, that you may proclaim the praises of Him who called you out of darkness into His marvelous light; who once were not a people but are now the people of God, who had not obtained mercy but now have obtained mercy."
2 Peter 2:9-10

MY PRAYER FOR TODAY:

Dear Heavenly Father,

There have been more people on this planet than I can comprehend: throughout history and every generation, people have come and gone, lived and died. Matthew 7:14 says that "narrow is the gate and difficult is the way which leads to life, and there are few who find it." Yet, because Jesus is the Good Shepherd, I have been led into everlasting life. Beyond that, Lord, You chose me to live this earthly life to point others to the Cross of Christ.

Father, stir within me a sense of magnitude for what it means to be chosen by You. It is not only a blessing and a privilege, Lord, it is a responsibility which I want to understand more fully. Cause me to live in a way that would bring glory to You and bear the fruit that you intend. I see through the scriptures that being chosen means You have a vested interest in my fruitfulness through this temporary life; one that should impact eternity. Therefore, I declare through the Holy Spirit that I am productive to an everlasting measure; that the little things I do, when accomplished in Your Name, produce great results for the Kingdom of God.

Cause my spiritual eyes to see that every circumstance creates a possibility for me to produce what You determine for each situation, Lord. I thank You for the call You have placed upon my life; may I continue to labor as one who will receive a full reward here in this life, and in the one to come. I pray these things in Jesus' Name. Amen!

FACETS

◊   Today, read Romans 8:29, 30 and take special note of the use of the words 'foreknew' and 'predestined.' Now, for contrast, read Matthew 7:21-23.

◊   According to these verses, what causes God to recognize that He "knows" us?

◊   We must always remember that it is God's will that everyone would come to the saving knowledge of Jesus Christ (1 Timothy 2:4). Be encouraged today that everyone whom the Holy Spirit places upon your heart to pray is someone whom God wants even more than you! Continue to intercede and lift up those who the Lord places in your life and thank Him in advance for salvation. Hallelujah!

◊   Write down the names of family members and friends for whom you are praying to receive Jesus Christ as their Savior. Please pray for them right now!

DAY 35
I AM JOYFUL

"You make known to me the path of life; you will fill me with joy in your presence, with eternal pleasures at your right hand."
Psalm 16:11

"The LORD is my strength and my shield; my heart trusts in him, and he helps me. My heart leaps for joy, and with my song I praise him."
Psalm 28:7

"Restore to me the joy of my salvation, and uphold me by your generous Spirit."
Psalm 51:12

"If you keep my commands, you will remain in my love, just as I have kept my Father's commands and remain in his love. I have told you this so that my joy may be in you and that your joy may be complete."
John 15:10-11

"Rejoice in the Lord always. Again I will say, rejoice!"
Philippians 4:4

MY PRAYER FOR TODAY:

Loving Father, Your word constantly encourages - even commands - me to be joyful. How can I not smile at the thought? You are not a distant, stoic, downcast God; in fact, You are one who persuades me to find joy especially through hardship, sufferings, and persecution. Who would know what better medicine to prescribe for a disheartened soul? Therefore, Lord, I declare to You that I am joyful, and will find even more joy when circumstances arise and people threaten to steal it away from me. I confess that this supernatural joy is not an emotion; it's a gift You gave me at the time of my salvation. Help me to understand this, Lord.

Just as You offered me eternal life, You also offered me the ability to experience great joy, even through the most difficult situations - perhaps even in spite of these situations! This is a gift I desire to use more fully, at every opportunity. I want to reflect this attribute of Jesus each day of my life. May I be a woman of God who attracts - not detracts - those who are searching for answers to their problems. Let my face be one that shines with the love of Jesus, and for my eyes to emit that beautiful light that manifests from within.

You are my strength, the sole source of my joy, and I will not allow man, the enemy, or situations overtake that which keeps me anchored to Your side. Your joy is invaluable; one that I treasure and will seek to keep before me daily. I love You so much, Lord!

FACETS

◊   The command to rejoice or to be joyful is repeated throughout the Bible. Our God isn't a sour grape! The concept of joy is also found as a running theme in the book of Psalms. David must have sang his heart out to God many times, searching for deep refreshing in the Lord.

◊   Have you ever pondered the difference between the words 'joy' and 'happiness?' Consider Paul and Silas in prison (Acts 16:25-26), singing to the Lord. What causes joy?

◊   Write a list of things that make you happy, then write a list of things that bring you joy. Do you find any differences? How about similarities? Write your observations below your list.

DAY 36
I AM INSEPARABLE FROM THE LOVE OF GOD

"And the LORD, He is the one who goes before you. He will be with you, He will not leave you nor forsake you; do not fear nor be dismayed."
Deuteronomy 31:8

"My sheep hear My voice, and I know them, and they follow Me. And I give them eternal life, and they shall never perish; neither shall anyone snatch them out of My hand. My Father, who has given them to Me, is greater than all; and no one is able to snatch them out of My Father's hand. I and My Father are one."
John 10:27-30

"For I am convinced that neither death nor life, neither angels nor demons, neither the present nor the future, nor any powers, neither height nor depth, nor anything else in all creation, will be able to separate us from the love of God that is in Christ Jesus our Lord."
Romans 8:38-39 KJV

MY PRAYER FOR TODAY:

Who is like You, God? Who is able to save a soul from torment and eternal pain; from the deepest anguish and heart-wrenching sorrow? No one, Lord. I declare that no one is capable, nor has there ever been, nor will there ever be. From before You established time on the earth, Your plan was always one of redemption. In Your infinite knowledge, You were aware of my faults, my mistakes, and my offenses before I was born, and yet You sent Jesus to bring me into fellowship with You through the perfect sacrifice at Calvary. Eternity isn't long enough to express my gratitude for this gift of salvation.

I thank You for the hope that I have in Jesus. Your Word convinces me that there is nothing that could separate me from Your love. With this truth in my heart, bearing witness to my spirit, how could I stray from you? Why would I choose to? I have my sights firmly fixed on You, my Heavenly Father; my heart is set on keeping Your Word and allowing it to transform me in every area of my life.

In those times of silence, Lord, remind me that You are near. In times of testing, cause me to focus on Your presence. Let me be mindful of this truth especially when circumstances tempt me to think otherwise. How grateful I am for the truth of Your Word and for Your unfailing love!

In Jesus' beautiful Name, I pray. Amen.

FACETS

◊   God's Word says He throws our sin as far as the east is from the west (Ps 103:12), and that He remembers them no more (Heb 8:12). What a striking contrast to Romans 8:38 and 39 which was part of our reading today!

◊   A patriot always identifies himself with his country; an activist identifies himself with his cause. What aspects of your life do you see as inseparable parts of your identity?

◊   If you have not given your life to Christ, reflect on your thoughts regarding today's devotional and write them here. Also, Lovely One, please visit page 184 where an invitation to meet Jesus is waiting for you!

DAY 37
I AM HIGHLY FAVORED

"Bless the Lord, O my soul,
And forget not all His benefits:
Who forgives all your iniquities,
Who heals all your diseases,
Who redeems your life from destruction,
Who crowns you with lovingkindness and tender mercies, Who
satisfies your mouth with good things,
So that your youth is renewed like the eagle's."
Psalm 103:2-5

"He who did not spare His own Son, but delivered Him up
for us all, how shall He not with Him also freely give us all
things?"
Romans 8:32

I DECLARE TODAY:

Dear Heavenly Father,

I am grateful for life. My life. I am blessed and highly favored. My enemies flee before my face, scattering seven ways. My Father causes me to ride over the heads of my accusers, and to remain free from the snares of lying tongues. My Lord causes those in my household to sleep in peace, for joy to come forth and for love to emanate from my home.

When He calls out to me, I answer. Those who belong to Him know the Shepherd's voice and they will not follow the voice of another. I now condemn every mouth that rises up against me, for this is my heritage in God my Deliverer. Who can curse whom the Lord has already blessed? I am blessed; therefore no curse or deceitful tongue may rise up against me and cause destruction.

I am a woman of passion, mercy, virtue, truth, and might. my Heavenly Father, and my Father alone – promotes and exalts. It is my Father's desire for love, power and wisdom and anointing to flow freely through my life. The grace of my God allows me to build my life upon the solid foundation of Jesus Christ. I grant the Holy Spirit full access into my heart and give Him permission to tear down and rebuild any areas as He sees fit. I willingly give the Lord Jesus all authority over my life.

I confess all this in His Name. Amen.

FACETS

◊   Jot down several instances in your life where you have clearly walked in the favor of the Lord. Sometimes we see God in an even bigger way when we can reflect on the little things he does for us. Big, small – simply praise the Lord for the ways which he personally displays his tender love toward you!

DAY 38

I AM BEAUTIFUL

"How beautiful on the mountains are the feet of the messenger bringing good news,
Breaking the news that all's well, proclaiming good times,
announcing salvation, telling Zion, 'Your God reigns!' "
Isaiah 52:7 The Message

"Do not let your adornment be merely outward—arranging the hair, wearing gold, or putting on fine apparel—rather let it be the hidden person of the heart, with the incorruptible beauty of a gentle and quiet spirit, which is very precious in the sight of God."
1 Peter 3:3-4

MY PRAYER FOR TODAY:

Lord, You do not make mistakes. Everything that You made You called good, and You are well pleased with Your creation. I am Yours; everything that I am I give to You. I give You my disappointments and every insecurity. I give You every corrupted thought that does not come from You or align with Your Word. I choose to renew my mind to Your truth. Before I was born, You knew me. As a child, You saw the person I am today. You even see the person I will be at the end of my years on earth. You have always loved me, and You see me as beautiful because I am Yours.

Father, give me Your eyes so that I may see myself according to Your truth alone. I refuse to allow Satan and his deceiving demons access into my mind; I will not believe the lies he has whispered to me in the past and will no longer entertain the thoughts he attempts to plant and desires to take root. His lies are not welcome and they cannot reside within my mind, the place I am renewing day by day by remaining in Your Word.

I thank You for the truth; I will no longer speak against myself, or tear myself down. Who am I to criticize what You call beautiful? Teach me to use my words in ways that will build and not destroy. You see so much more than my natural eyes can see. Help me to understand Your definition of the word "beautiful." I make a commitment now and choose to look beyond the world's definition. I desire only to identify myself in the way that You see me. Help me to grasp the depth and the richness of that word! I declare right now that I am beautiful; I am wonderfully made! You are pleased with Your creation, Your daughter!

I praise You for Your mighty works and the work You are doing right now in me. In Jesus' Name. Amen.

FACETS

◊   It's absolutely no revelation that the world is fixated on outward appearances. Standards of beauty around the world are shaped by culture, and of course, has transformed throughout the ages. Consider the following historical fact regarding the Edo Period of Japan:

In the 19th century women painted their teeth black, a custom that was considered to make them attractive. Women painted their teeth with a layer of logwood, a dye made with rice vinegar and pieces of iron and was the same material use to make the base for Japanese lacquerware. Women shaved their eyebrows and blackened teeth, some believe, to hide their natural expression. *

◊   Research two or three different cultural periods of various countries and write down your most interesting findings. It's easy to see that we must view ourselves according to God's standard and not the world, for the things of the world truly shift and fade.

*Taken from factsanddetails.com, Japan / Life and Culture in the Edo Period.

DAY 39
I AM HIS BELOVED

"Show Your marvelous lovingkindness by Your right hand,
O You who save those who trust in You
From those who rise up against them.
Keep me as the apple of Your eye;
Hide me under the shadow of Your wings..."
Psalm 17:7-8

"How precious also are Your thoughts to me, O God!
How great is the sum of them!
If I should count them, they would be more in
number than the sand;
When I awake, I am still with You."
Psalm 139:17-18

MY PRAYER FOR TODAY:

Dear Heavenly Father,

Nothing on earth could compare with the love I have in You, Lord. Nothing of greater worth exists; no greater stature could I ever obtain than being one You call Your very own. There are no riches, no gain, no favor that can match the value of being Your daughter.

There are those who have used Your Word for their own gain and their own glory; there are those who attempt to expound on Your Word through their limited perception in the flesh. Those are the ones who preach that You are a god of injustice, or a god of hatred. Those who make these proclamations do not know the True and Living God. I know You as the One who holds my life in Your hands. I know You as the Lover of my soul and the Keeper of my heart. You are my God — the One who calls me the apple of His eye; the One who tells me to cast all my cares upon You, for You care for me. You are the God who constantly thinks precious thoughts of me!

Thank You for this indescribably rich love. I proclaim it is mine, in Jesus' Name. Amen!

FACETS

◊ Today, draw a picture of how you imagine God's love toward you. It can be anything at all - whatever comes to your heart. If you prefer, create a collage taken from different images you find in magazines, books, anywhere. Just be creative!

DAY 40
I AM FREE

"The Spirit of the Lord GOD is upon me; because the LORD hath anointed me to preach good tidings unto the meek; he hath sent me to bind up the brokenhearted, to proclaim liberty to the captives, and the opening of the prison to them that are bound; to proclaim the acceptable year of the LORD, and the day of vengeance of our God; to comfort all that mourn; to appoint unto them that mourn in Zion, to give unto them beauty for ashes, the oil of joy for mourning, the garment of praise for the spirit of heaviness; that they might be called trees of righteousness, the planting of the LORD, that he might be glorified."
Isaiah 61:1-3

"Therefore, there is now no condemnation for those who are in Christ Jesus, because through Christ Jesus the law of the Spirit who gives life has set me free from the law of sin and death."
Romans 8:1-2

"If the Son therefore shall make you free, ye shall be free indeed."
John 8:36 KJV

I DECLARE TODAY:

I was once bound and captive to sin in a life that, at one time, did not honor and glorify God. I remember the bondage of what it was like to serve myself and to obey the lusts of my flesh. It is good to remember in order that I may hold at the forefront of my mind the freedom that Christ came to give me. Because Jesus freed me through His death and resurrection, I no longer remain a captive to sin. I am made alive unto God and I am free because the Son has set me free indeed! I am free because I am grasping the fullness of my salvation. I realize that God did not liberate me from a life of sin in order that I might live again simply for myself. I declare that I am free, unhindered by the fear of man, unrestrained of my intense devotion and love for my Savior, unmoved by circumstances that can change and sway daily.

My freedom was won by God Himself, and given to me when I believed and received Jesus as my Redeemer. I choose to operate in the light and truth of that freedom by walking in love, and living out a life of joy. My freedom is precious and I have decided to serve my God wholly by embracing it and living in such a way that gives no place to fear and condemnation. I am free because I live a life that exudes love; I am free because I choose to grasp the perfect love that Jesus bore on the Cross for me. His perfect love casts fear out of my life. I declare the truth of God's Word that I have not been given a spirit of fear, but of love, power, and a sound mind. God's love, power, and strength enable me to walk in absolute freedom! I bind all oppression and lies that would come against the truth and knowledge of God's best for me, and I loose my heart and mind, submitting them to my Heavenly Father that I might be continually transformed into His image and likeness.

I thank You for the precious freedom I have in Jesus. May this freedom be seen by all as a holy display of love, respect, and devotion I have to my beautiful Savior. Amen.

FACETS

I wrote this several years ago as a blog article. I was so captivated by this little boy and that picture of freedom, I never wanted to forget the impact that it made on my heart.

LETTING GO OF THE HANDLEBARS

"Now the Lord is the Spirit; and where the Spirit of the Lord is, there is liberty." 2 Cor 3:17

When I hear the word "freedom," the same image always comes to mind. It's a picture of a little boy blazing down a steep hill on his bike, hands raised above his head in complete defiance to caution and the threat of gravitational consequences. This is what I saw one morning as I drove my usual route to work. I became aware of the Lord's presence so strongly the instant I saw that boy, my heart began racing. Captivated by the scene, I heard the Lord speak to my spirit. "This is how I want My children to live in Me."

I want to live this kind of life in Christ: to never fear letting go of the handlebars and raising my arms up high as I move forward, putting all my trust in Him.

"But we all, with unveiled face, beholding as in a mirror the glory of the Lord, are being transformed into the same image from glory to glory, just as by the Spirit of the Lord." 2 Cor 3:18

◊   For your last Facet, consider what freedom looks like to you. Share it here and look back on it often!

A JEWEL FOR ETERNITY

You've made it! Congratulations on completing your 40-day mining expedition. :-) Did you get a glimpse of how much you mean to the God of the universe? Do you see how absolutely valuable you are to Him, and how you were created to make an earthly impact that will last throughout eternity? It is my prayer that not only are you viewing yourself in a brighter light, but most of all, that you've come to see the Lord Jesus anew. He is shining ever brighter and brighter upon you, and don't ever forget that! He above all is worthy of praise and glory. If you found yourself at any time during these past 40 days pausing during your devotions to praise God for what He has done, or simply sitting in silence in awe of His presence, then I couldn't be more joyful about your experience!

I want to encourage you to continue something which you began 40 days ago, and that is to practice regular prayer journaling. Now, I'm not talking about setting up a rigid and regimented obligation - I'm suggesting you just keep a journal handy so that, when the Spirit leads, you can continue conversations with, and give praises to, God. Of course, this would be *in addition* to your regular prayer time! Prayer journaling is a tangible record of God's faithfulness to you. How wonderful it is to look back and recall with such clarity those times when dark moments turned to dawn because of the Lord's intervention. I can't tell you how often I've read through certain passages of old journals, sometimes years later, that have provided comfort as I was awaiting yet another victory. Remembering our testimony gives us confidence in God's Word and helps us to focus on HIM, not our circumstances.

This book was born out of a hunger to communicate deeply with the Lord, and to put to remembrance His goodness. The prayers in this journal have been my very own prayers as well. Each one has come during a time when I have personally needed the Lord's clarity on who I am in Him. Having the ability to look back on times of need as well as times of rescue provides powerful, personal ministry. I'm reminded that even King David had to "encourage himself in the Lord" (*1 Samuel 30:6 KJV*) during times of distress and hardship.

REMEMBERING IS GOOD

As a mother of young girls (well, rather, young *ladies* now), I can't tell you how many times I've told both my daughters the same things, over and over again, until I felt like my lips were going numb! If you have children, no doubt you understand what I mean. Maybe you are constantly telling your kids to clean up after themselves at the dinner table, or to put away their shoes. Maybe you're forever reminding them to finish their homework or call you when they get home from school. Sometimes our children forget things we've said; perhaps they actually didn't hear us the first time (or the second time, OR the third time!). But aren't we like that as well? How often does our Heavenly Father need to remind us about how good He is, and that we can trust Him, and that we really are lovely in His sight?

Putting spiritual victories to remembrance is an invaluable weapon. We overcome the evil one by the blood of Jesus and the word of our testimony *(Rev 12:11)*. Look back often on what the Lord has accomplished in you through these last 40 days. Don't forget how He has spoken to your heart. Don't forget that He blesses His Word, and that when you speak it, you're agreeing with what is already blessed. Continue to lift Jesus above all else: circumstances, opinions, ideas, plans, thoughts, expectations - place Him above it all, and you will continue to see yourself as He already sees you - not as a diamond in the rough, but a priceless, eternal, radiant beauty of a gem!

AN INVITATION

Precious One, as you have journeyed through these days, I've been praying throughout the writing of this book that you would turn to this page. It is my hope that your eyes have been opened to the overwhelming love and delight that God Himself has for you. Whether you have never given your heart to Christ, or if you are returning to him after some time away, please take this moment to pray and accept the Lord's invitation into receiving a new life through Him.

PRAYER

Dear Jesus,

I have come to know that Your forgiveness is available to me. I understand, that You came to this earth in order to pay the price for my sins that would forever separate me from God. I also believe that You rose from the dead and live today. I confess my sins to You and turn away from them, and invite You to reside within my heart. I receive in faith this gift of salvation. Thank You for giving me a new heart and a new spirit, and for accepting me into Your eternal kingdom. Help me to live for You.

In Jesus' Name I pray. Amen.

SCRIPTURE INDEX

SCRIPTURE INDEX

1DAYJAPAN.COM
JAPAN MISSIONS FOCUS

Japan needs Jesus! And this is the reason we created 1dayjapan.com, a web site dedicated to teaching, encouraging, and collaborating to help bring the Good News of the gospel to the Japanese. By providing updated information regarding various facets of Japan missions, we feel it is a good way to unite in prayer and to help educate others.

21st century Japan is yet affected by bondages of the past. By providing an outlet of information for those not involved in Japan missions, it opens the windows of heaven just a bit more, as an invitation to prayer and mediation for considering Japan's greatest need -- hope in Jesus Christ alone!

JIM & TRACY XAVIER

along with their two daughters, serve as full-time missionaries in southern Japan on the island of Kyushu. Japan is a unique mission field in that the nation itself is modern and materially abundant. The Japanese lifestyle is one of hard work and very little rest, which puts a high premium on the value of time and solid relationships. Please pray that God would richly supply laborers, creativity, and finances for reaching the Japanese.

"STICKING UP" FOR JESUS

Being a Christian in a 99% non-Christian nation causes one to "stick up." One of the saddest yet most prevalent of Japanese proverbs states, "The nail that sticks up gets hammered back in." This means all must conform and those who do not will be put back into place by force, usually by way of intimidation from others and fear of being cast out of their important social and family circles. Of all challenges to the gospel, helping people make a solid commitment to Christ and the help of the Holy Spirit is what will bring Japan to Jesus, one by one.

BE A PART OF JAPAN'S SALVATION

We invite you to become a prayer partner with us! Visit 1dayjapan.com often or find us on Facebook. And if you are able, we encourage you to prayerfully consider becoming a financial sponsor of the work being done in this nation. Contact information is found below. God bless you, and please agree with us for a great harvest of souls here in Japan!

CONTACT

Website: http://1dayjapan.com
Email: info@1dayjapan.com

Japan Church Address:
2-26-24 Sue
Munakata City
Fukuoka Prefecture
811-4184 JAPAN
munakatabethel.com

US Church Address:
For financial giving:
10615 SE 216th St.
Kent, WA 98031
(253) 859-0832
riveroflifefellowship.org

THE WOMEN OF JAPAN NEED THIS BOOK.

Ministry to Japanese women is a necessity, not only because of the staggeringly small percentage of Christians in this nation, but because the culture bears a unique weight upon them, leaving many to feel insignificant, inadequate, fearful, and alone.

Please refer this book to your friends, your church members, or a woman who may need a fresh touch from God. When people purchase *Diamond in the Rough*, they will be helping to cover the costs of language translation and the initial printing of this book in Japanese. It is imperative that these lovely women find peace and passion for life, and to see themselves living out with great purpose. With your help, putting this book in their hands will not go unaccomplished.

How beautiful upon the mountains
are the feet of him who brings good news,
who publishes peace, who brings good news
of happiness, who publishes salvation,
who says to Zion, "Your God reigns."
- Isaiah 52:7 ESV

River of Life Fellowship
c/o Japan Missions
10615 SE 216th Street
Kent, WA 98031
(253) 859-0832

THE SOUND OF HEAVEN

You'd miss the joint if you weren't familiar with the area, and familiar we were not. We passed it at least twice as we zoomed back and forth on the same stretch of road for several minutes. Finally, we spotted the modest concrete brick building situated quite literally, under train tracks, and slipped in with just enough time to grab a few seats near the back. We were there to support our friend, Michiko, who sings in a gospel group called  New Wings. Apparently, from what I learned tonight, this was the group's showcase debut, and this unassuming club called The Beat Station served as their first major public venue, outside of their regular circuit of schools, nursing homes, and churches.

I hadn't been in a club for years. Now, sitting in the smoke-filled room among beer-sipping patrons with my pre-teen daughters was…different. As we waited for the performers to take their place on stage, I scanned the crowd, taking note of their demeanor, their eyes, expressions. There were many in support of either a friend or relative in the group, but mostly the patrons consisted of what I imagine were 'regulars,' or those who perhaps frequented any number of neighboring establishments.

Now, I have to give you a little background into the gospel music trend here in Japan. I'm certainly no expert on the matter, but what I can tell you is that it was introduced to Japan in the 1950's and lived on through the 1990's, when the *Sister Act* movies came out. That's when gospel exploded into a nationwide phenomenon. Gospel music (though not exclusively) is taught in secular settings and is a popular genre here among young and old alike. This fact may explain why, here at The Beat Station, this youthful crowd was gathered, anxious to hear and see what was to come.

I sensed great purpose as I was drawn to my feet, hearing not simply the sound of a trained gospel choir group, but the sound of heaven reaching down into the midst of the crowd and moving far beyond the boundaries of The Beat Station's concrete walls. I've been told that many who participate in gospel choir groups do not have an understanding of what they're singing because much of it is in English. And although many Japanese know or speak some English, many (if not most) do not have full comprehension of what they're hearing or saying when listening to or singing American gospel music. This, my friends, is miraculous in light of what God is preparing to pour out onto this nation.

Japan is a nation with a population of less than 2% Christian, with a rich history of flourishing Christianity in the late 1500's. Officially banned in 1626, **this percentage has remained relatively static for over 400 years.** Aware of this historical truth, my spirit soared in that little club last night, as Isaiah 55:10-11 burned in my heart.

> *"For as the rain comes down, and the snow from heaven,*
> *And do not return there,*
> *But water the earth,*
> *And make it bring forth and bud,*
> *That it may give seed to the sower*
> *And bread to the eater,*
> *So shall My word be that goes forth from My mouth;*
> *It shall not return to Me void,*
> *But it shall accomplish what I please,*
> *And it shall prosper in the thing for which I sent it."*

The Word of the Lord was repeatedly, powerfully, and excellently proclaimed by this beautiful group of young people for over two hours. Regardless of what was comprehended in the natural, God's declaration over the nation was pouring forth from the realm of the eternal. God's Word, like seed, has been planted, protected, watered, and nurtured for over 400 years in Japan. I believe we are preparing to see not only the fruit that will result from this seed, but we are preparing to see the mighty tree from which it will grow.

192

NOTES

Made in the USA
Charleston, SC
29 November 2012